Kickstart Your Money

0

Kickstart Your Money

The Complete Guide to Managing Your Personal Finances

Rachel Fixsen

JOHN WILEY & SONS, LTD

Other Wiley Editorial Offices

John Wiley & Sons, Inc., 605 Third Avenue,
New York, NY 10158–0012, USA

WILEY-VCH Verlag GmbH, Pappelallee 3,
D-69469 Weinheim, Germany

John Wiley & Sons Australia Ltd, 33 Park Road, Milton,
Queensland 4064, Australia

John Wiley & Sons (Asia) Pte Ltd, 2 Clementi Loop #02–01,
Jin Xing Distripark, Singapore 129809

John Wiley & Sons (Canada) Ltd, 22 Worcester Road,
Rexdale, Ontario M9W 1L1, Canada

British Library Cataloguing in Publication Data

A catalogue record for this book is available from the British Library

ISBN 0–470–84366–7

Typeset in New Caledonia by Florence Production Ltd, Stoodleigh, Devon.
Printed and bound in Great Britain by Biddles Ltd, Guildford and King's Lynn.
This book is printed on acid-free paper responsibly manufactured from sustainable forestry, in which at least two trees are planted for each one used for paper production.

Contents

About the Author

Rachel Fixsen is a freelance financial journalist who writes regularly for national newspapers including *The Independent* and *The Observer*, and magazines *Moneywise* and *Investment & Pensions Europe*. She specializes in writing on personal finance and investment issues.

She spent many years working abroad, holding jobs in Copenhagen, Berlin and Cologne during her years as a student. In the year leading up to the fall of the Berlin Wall, she studied at Leipzig University, writing about her experiences of life under the old regime when she returned to London.

In 1993, she worked for Reuters as a correspondent in Frankfurt. There she jointly set up and ran Frankfurt's first foreign journalists club – The International Business Journalists Forum of Frankfurt. The club invited prominent speakers from the financial community including two Bundesbank presidents.

After leaving Frankfurt, she moved to New York where she worked as an editor for Reuters. Having re-settled in England in 1996, she now lives in the South Gloucestershire village of Hawkesbury Upton with her two young children Jack and Kitty.

Introduction

Many people just assume that if you are good at your job you must therefore be excellent at organizing your personal life too. Your CDs are surely filed in alphabetical order, you always discard tins in your kitchen cupboard when they pass their sell-by date, and of course you pay meticulous attention to your personal money matters.

But the fact is that many people who are really dedicated to their work focus all their attention and energy on the professional side of their lives. They then end up having scant resources left over to manage their private affairs. They may keep no record of the amount they spend on their credit card or neglect being up-to-date with checking their bank statements.

It is all very well to spend most of your energy actually earning money. But managing your personal finances is essential too. If your private money matters are at all precarious, this mismanagement is in danger of undermining your own efforts at work.

For instance, if you get weighed down with credit card debt, the ensuing problems will preoccupy you and could easily hamper your performance in your career. At worst you could end up unwittingly overspending and find yourself unable to pay off loans and credit card bills, even if you are a high earner.

This book covers all major aspects of personal finance, and speaks specifically to those who are serious about planning their careers. If you are planning your future career, you are clearly not afraid to look ahead. You know all too well that decisions you make today may have a great impact on the years ahead.

This book aims to show you why it is important to take control of your personal finances as early as possible in your career, and it gives you the knowledge to enable you to do so effectively. It is meant for people of all ages who are keen to make a new start with their own money matters.

To get your money matters well and truly set up for the future, you need to gain a broad knowledge of the financial products which are available to you and how they work. But you also need the motivation to put your plans into action. Hopefully, this book will galvanize your good intentions by clearly setting out the reasons for making provision for the future, and explaining the value of starting long-term investment early.

Budgeting is a vital part of managing your money. But for many it is also one of the most tricky bits of the whole jigsaw. While putting a regular monthly sum into an investment scheme happens automatically once you have made the decision to go ahead, keeping your spending within limits is an exercise which requires almost hourly self-discipline.

It is not just how you spend your money but how you earn it that will determine how wealthy you are. So this book takes a look at your income too, and shows how you can keep it high, albeit within the limits of your chosen career path.

The art of negotiation is critical here. Even the most competent and well-informed employee can miss out on a salary rise if they fail to notice that their boss is having a bad day when they broach the subject.

Before you can make reliable decisions on your financial future, you need to define your aims. This means you have to look confidently to the future and try to imagine possible and likely scenarios ahead of you.

Use this book to do this and you will then feel more committed to the financial arrangements you put in place for the future. There is no point in starting ambitious regular savings plans if two months later you stop contributing, and can't remember why it seemed so important to take them out in the first place.

You will learn to make your own decisions about investments rather than relying on the vast pool of financial advisers out there. Financial advisers can be a very useful source of information, but many are basically salesmen for products and services from certain providers, and few are able to give the truly independent advice you require to make an informed choice. Bank managers are also no longer the altruistic figures of old – if ever they were. They again may have a vested interest in selling you selected products and services.

This book will help you find your own financial feet, as well as giving guidance on indentifying the right places to find independent, unbiased advice.

Acknowledgements

Many thanks to all the people and organizations who helped me research this book, including Julie Lord of Cavendish Financial Management in Cardiff; John Ions of SG Asset Management; Kevin Minter of the David Aaron Partnership; Des Hamilton of the Occupational Pensions Advisory Service; Donna Bradshaw of Fiona Price and Partners in London; the press offices of the Department for Work and Pensions, the Financial Services Authority and the Inland Revenue; Neil Mainland at Financial Dynamics; Nick Fixsen; Bina Abel of Bradford and Bingley; Kim North of Pretty Technical Partnership; the press office at William Mercer; and Scott Cromar at PricewaterhouseCoopers.

Chapter 1

Maximizing Your Salary

Most money advice is focused on how to spend, save, invest or otherwise use up the money you have coming in. The assumption often seems to be that while your income is fixed, your expenditure is flexible. Controlling this side of the equation is often seen as the key to successful financial organization.

This is true to a large extent, and for many people there is nothing they can reasonably do to increase the income they have. But if you are lucky enough to be in good health, resourceful and motivated, your income is not as immutable as you might think. When you make an initial decision on which career path to embark on, this is a major financial choice.

Of course your primary consideration when making this choice is which type of daily activity would give you the most satisfaction. You also have to choose an occupation for which you have the skills or the aptitude – nothing is going to work if you are not capable of doing the job or so bored by it that you cannot motivate yourself to engage your brain while in the confines of the workplace.

But depending on the area of work you choose, you will probably still be left with some leeway on how much you can earn. Think laterally, and consider all the options.

For example, if your chosen profession is nursing, think strategically about your career options from the financial point of view. How much choice will you have in a few years' time? You could stay in mainstream nursing, or become specialized.

You could choose to enter private medicine, either as a clinic nurse or for paying patients.

As a mental health nurse, for example, you could aim to train to become a psychotherapist. From a financial point of view, this move could result in you earning perhaps twice the amount you are paid as a senior nurse.

If you study to be a solicitor, you are likely to earn a good salary as almost any type of solicitor. But lawyers working for large City firms specializing in commercial law take home around twice as much as solicitors practising law in the provinces.

Consider all the lifestyle implications of each choice carefully. Think ahead – will you need training, further qualifications or specific job experience to help you achieve a particular aim ten years ahead? How will you finance this?

How much does your profession pay?

So if you are still in the stage before you have committed yourself to a long-term career – or if you are in the process of giving up your current career in favour of a new path – you are in a good position to set your own income according to how much money you want to have.

When you start to consider careers, always make sure you are well informed about how much that type of job pays, and what the range is. Find out what the range means by asking: are the highest levels of pay in that particular profession earned only by the top 10 professionals in the country? Or are these top levels of pay earned by anyone who works in our expensive capital city?

Talk to people about it. The very best way to research the realities of the line of work you have chosen is to identify a

Average annual salaries for different jobs

General managers and administrators in national and local government, large companies and organizations	£33,781
Production managers in manufacturing, construction, mining and energy industries	£33,921
Treasurers and company financial managers	£62,583
Marketing and sales managers	£40,521
Purchasing managers	£40,521
Advertising and public relations managers	£37,860
Computer systems and data processing managers	£40,884
Financial institution and office managers, civil service executive officers	£27,002
Police officers (inspector and above)	£43,703
Farm owners and managers	£20,834
Restaurant and catering managers	£18,014
Chemists	£29,329
Biological scientists and biochemists	£27,451
Engineers and technologists	£30,044
Medical practitioners	£54,353
University and polytechnic teaching professionals	£33,037
Secondary education teaching professionals	£26,216
Primary and nursery education teaching professionals	£24,191

Solicitors	£40,610
Chartered and certified accountants	£31,444
Architects	£29,451
Librarians	£22,268
Psychologists	£30,953
Clergy	£15,768
Social workers	£21,093
Scientific technicians	£21,946
Computer analysts/programmers	£28,422
Nurses	£20,683
Midwives	£24,123
Authors, writers, journalists	£29,498
Photographers, camera operators	£21,400

Source: Office for National Statistics, New Earnings Survey 2000

professional who has spent several years in that particular business. By letter or email, simply introduce yourself and ask if you may pick their brains for the general information you want. That person may be too busy to give you the answers you need, so don't forget to ask them for the contact details of someone else who may be able to help if they themselves don't have enough time.

Professional bodies or industry associations are a good source of information.

Even if a high income is not one of your career priorities, it still is worth considering right at the start what the options will be within your chosen profession for higher pay.

After all, you never know how your priorities could change over the years. Perhaps world travel – or another expensive hobby – will become more important to you in a decade's time. If you are stuck in a career with few options to increase your earnings power, your might later be forced to retrain for a new career – an expensive and time-consuming process, not to mention a mid-life crisis in the making.

Think long-term

Although this book focuses on money, if you are to manage your career successfully, you need to consider your salary level in a medium-term perspective. Don't be tempted to go at all costs for the highest salary in the short term. It is often worth thinking strategically by gathering essential skills in a lower-paid job at first. Or making a carefully considered return to higher education – and putting up with being poverty-stricken for a while – should enhance your long-term earnings potential.

Look at yourself from an employer's point of view. Are you improving as an overall package? To a certain extent your remuneration will take care of itself if you simply concentrate on doing your job well.

Typically, it is junior employees in large organizations who are prepared to move from one company to another for the sake of a marginal increase in salary. But if you stick with this approach in the longer term, it could be detrimental in overall career terms. You will never build up a relationship of trust within one organization.

You need to set realistic goals in your career, and if you end up moving in the short term, you cannot really satisfy those goals.

Rather than being totally driven by immediate salary levels, you should also place a value on your job – and determine what it means for you, and how it will benefit you in the long term.

Negotiating your salary

As a potential new employee in a company, whether you have been headhunted or you are applying for a job, the people marketing the job will already have an idea of the salary range they are prepared to offer you.

You will be asked to disclose your current salary. If your application succeeds, you will be offered a remuneration package that improves upon your present salary but is within their range.

You could always pull the wool over your new employer's eyes by exaggerating your current salary in order to be offered a higher starting-level pay. But it is not worth doing this. It is altogether likely that this will come to light and the deception would undoubtedly be very damaging for you.

But before you are interviewed for any job, it helps to find out what the going rate for such a position is. If you are staying in the same line of work, start by asking contacts and colleagues for information.

Publications that carry recruitment advertising can help, as many advertisements state the level of salary that will be offered.

If you know a headhunter or recruitment consultant, they can be a useful source of information as they will have access to salary scales.

If there is to be a negotiation process for a new job – and provided the job is at a fairly high level – this is often more effective if conducted through a third party, such as a recruitment consultant or even a lawyer.

This leaves you free to concentrate on selling yourself and your skills. The details of a remuneration package such as share options, company car, etc. can seem too personal to discuss comfortably with a future employer face to face.

However, it all depends on your personality. If you have a clear idea of exactly what it is you want, then you may feel more in control doing the negotiating directly.

Once in your job, you will probably have an annual salary review on a more or less formal basis. To what extent this is negotiable depends on your employer. In the civil service, for example, there are set salary bandings for each job. There is a degree of negotiation within those bands, based on your competencies. But you can't negotiate a salary that is outside the band for your particular job.

In the public sector too, employers have very tight budget constraints and are often simply not able to offer more. In the private sector at least, there should always be scope for negotiating your salary – provided that you make a valuable contribution in terms of work.

Of course you can have a better quality of life with more money in your pocket, but this is not the only reason why it is in your interests to keep your salary at a relatively high level. As long as you are good at your job, your salary level will serve to remind your managers that you are a valuable member of staff and keep you uppermost in their minds when a promotion is up for grabs.

Also, if you should change jobs, your current salary will give new employers an instant measure of how highly valued you were by your previous bosses.

Remind your boss how much you are worth

Women are still paid much less than men. According to a study by the Equal Opportunities Commission (EOC), 30 years after the Equal Pay Act, women are still taking home only four-fifths of men's earnings. This is the largest pay gap between the sexes in the European Union.

Recruitment consultants report that women are not as ready as men to blow their own trumpets, and this old-fashioned modesty does not help them increase their earnings. In today's companies, the onus is on the employee to remind their boss just how much they are worth to the business, so women are often at a disadvantage because of their emotional predisposition to reticence.

So perhaps it is particularly important for women to improve their negotiating skills and to learn to become more comfortable in asserting their value to the company.

Your boss will be more convinced that you warrant a pay rise if they are presented with a list of your achievements. And the more concrete these are the better. You will be in a very good position if you can actually point to numbers of new clients you have brought in or increases in sales you have overseen.

It is worth keeping a diary during the year of achievements as they occur to remind you when the time for a pay review comes around.

If you are to negotiate your salary successfully, it is important to retain a picture of how others in your company are paid. In some companies – and particularly in public sector jobs such as the police – how others are paid is public knowledge. But more typically in the private sector, this is information which is closely guarded by both management and often the employees themselves.

If this is the case, the best sources of information are friendly colleagues and general gossip in the office. Be willing to disclose your salary to friends in the office, and they will probably be willing to tell you theirs. This knowledge is useful, but obviously avoid betraying this confidence by citing others' salaries to management in your negotiations.

Otherwise, web site www.workthing.com has a salary checker. You simply have to enter your job description and location, and the web site will produce the average salary and highest for your job.

Remember that your remuneration is not simply your annual gross salary. Other benefits come into the package. A good occupational pension, for example, can be worth a great deal (see Chapter 4).

Incentives such as share option schemes can also bump your financial rewards up significantly, although these returns are unpredictable. There are numerous other possible benefits ranging from private medical insurance to company cars and golf club membership.

Keep a close eye on alternative job opportunities, even if you are happy working where you are. You need to get a fair picture of how much your skills and experience are worth in the employment market. There may be a competitor firm where you could easily find a job. Perhaps members of staff from your company have been poached by another business or have come from another firm.

Be tactful

When it comes to approaching your boss or line manager for a pay review, tact and diplomacy are of utmost importance. Nobody wants to work with someone who appears obsessed with their level of salary. It can give the impression that the actual work you do is unimportant.

Be aware when you are due to have a salary review. One month before this date, approach your boss to ask for an appointment to speak to them about the subject. Choose a quiet moment when they appear to be in a positive mood.

A casual request for a chat with your boss at the end of a quiet day is ideal. But pick your moment in terms of how you are viewed at work. If your office is still reeling from the effects of a huge error you have just made, then any request for more pay may not be just fruitless, but may focus attention all the more sharply on your failings.

Prepare yourself well for the meeting. When you speak to your boss, try to take control of the meeting, but do so sensitively.

Tell your boss – assertively but not belligerently – what your achievements and contributions have been, and what you will contribute in the future. Provide your boss with good and clear arguments for a pay rise that they can relay if necessary to higher management.

Then give a figure for the new salary you believe would be appropriate. Try to be realistic, because if you name a figure which is clearly too high, you will undermine your credibility.

Keep the tone of the meeting friendly, firm and unthreatening. Do not give the impression that you would be prepared to seek another job if you don't get what you want.

However, if you feel you are undervalued at your company, and you have been thwarted in your attempts to have your salary increased to the level you feel your contribution warrants, then it may be time to take a more formal approach. In larger companies, you can lodge a request for a pay rise with the personnel or human resources department.

Get another job offer

If you are in this situation and you have other grievances about the job you do, then your best move would probably be to look for another job.

But if you are happy where you are, if only you were rewarded more highly, then you may need to show your boss what you would be worth elsewhere.

After thorough research, approach another company for a job, preferably through a contact at the firm. When you have a firm job offer, ask for an appointment with your boss.

Tell them politely about your offer, and make it clear that you would far prefer to stay with your current employer. It is just that you feel you are not valued enough. Again, give clear and concise reasons why you are worth the salary you are requesting.

Watch out, though, because this is a dangerous game to play. After all, if it turns out you are not valued at your company, you may simply be encouraged to take the new job. So try to make it clear to your boss that you would prefer to stay put. If you do this, then it will still be possible for you – even if your salary request is turned down – to keep your job without losing face.

If, however, you give your boss an ultimatum, then you will really have to take up the other job offer.

Using the tactic of soliciting another job offer to gain leverage with your current employer can taint your reputation in the long term with your company, but you can probably get away with doing it once.

Chapter 2

Managing Your Own Money Effectively

Make good money management a priority

Being able to manage the financial side of your personal life effectively is a vital skill. If you learnt control over your money matters early on in life, then you are one of the lucky ones.

Many adults suffer because their finances somehow seem to run away with them. They overspend, fail to make important payments and can end up in serious difficulties. Left untreated, financial problems can end up affecting nearly every area of your life.

For example, if you are in desperate need of cash you may be tempted to falsify expense claims at work – a move which will cost you your job if discovered. Relationships frequently break down over money. Once one partner starts concealing a shortage of cash this can snowball until massive joint debts are incurred without the other partner's knowledge.

But money skills can be learnt, even if you started off on the wrong foot as a student. You need to give this part of your life a high priority and you need to equip yourself with the necessary knowledge to find your way around the financial services maze.

First steps to getting organized

You also need to set aside a time – several evenings or two full days – to put your personal finances on a stable footing. And then you need to make a regular appointment in your schedule

– perhaps once a week – to pay bills, log activity in your bank account and assess whether your spending is within budget.

Talk to someone about it

When you first start getting your personal money matters in order, it is a good idea to make an appointment with a financial adviser. Make it clear to them that you are only making initial enquiries about what sort of products they think you need, so that you don't feel obliged to buy anything just yet.

So at this point it doesn't matter whether you see an independent financial adviser or an agent tied to one particular financial services provider.

It is very helpful to talk things over with someone, and all qualified financial advisers should know the major products in the market and be able to give you some idea of your options and the cost.

But think about it on your own first. What are your needs? What risks are you worried about, and which disasters do you think you could cope with financially? Reading through the rest of this chapter will guide you through the main areas you might need to consider.

Budgeting

Drawing up a realistic budget is a very useful exercise, and one that you should repeat every year, or at least after any significant change in your life, such as a house move, marriage, the birth of children or a new job.

Be realistic, not optimistic

As long as you have a reasonable level of income, setting out a budget for personal spending does not have to be a controlling exercise. The whole thing would be counterproductive if you gave yourself unrealistically low spending levels which you then hoped you would keep to.

The point is to give yourself an accurate picture of how much money you need to spend to have the lifestyle you are happy with – obviously within reason!

How to cut your spending

But if you know you are overspending, then now is the time to look carefully at your realistic budget and consider where you can cut your spending. There is a real art to this. You have to have a good degree of self-knowledge and be honest with yourself about spending cuts which you could stick to. If you set goals you don't manage to keep to, this will make you feel out of control and demoralized – a state of mind that could well draw you into deeper trouble.

If you are a smoker, for example, don't bank on being able to give up just to save money. Getting to grips with an addiction is not a simple matter.

If you set limits on areas of your spending that you rely on emotionally, you may end up feeling deprived when you are having a bad day and then rebel from your self-imposed rule. So without going into therapy to discover why you are emotionally dependent on, for example, treating yourself to new underwear every week, it is best to avoid cutting spending on these items.

Keep it painless

But most people on at least an average income will find there is some spending they can almost painlessly cut out. If you regularly buy takeaway food rather than cooking at home, this is an easy habit to change. And the taste of even the simplest home-cooked food should be enough of an improvement in your quality of life to compensate for the lost convenience.

Perhaps you are very generous in your gifts to friends and people you visit. But consider the cost. Bringing a good bottle of wine and flowers to a host twice a week could cost £120 a month. Of course it is nice to give, and fine if you can easily afford it, but no true friend would want you to spend money on them that you need yourself.

How could you cut your spending?

- Use public transport instead of your own car
- Use a bicycle instead of car or public transport
- Eat out less often
- Eat out at less-expensive restaurants
- Drink at pubs rather than wine bars
- Buy fewer or less-expensive clothes
- Take a packed lunch to work rather than buying lunch in town
- Drive a car that costs less to insure
- Use your mobile phone less
- Cut down on telephone use
- Switch Internet service providers

- Impose a cooling-off period on yourself before making major purchases
- Reduce electricity usage through awareness
- Avoid car-parking fees by parking in free areas and walking to the shops
- Switch your mortgage to a cheaper provider.

Once you have drawn up a realistic budget – and ideally given it a test run for two months – you will know how much money you have left over every month for medium- and long-term savings and any insurance premiums.

Remember – you are doing this for yourself

Sticking to a budget – even if it is generous – requires some degree of self-discipline. Discipline is a harsh word, and for many the term self-discipline conjures up an image of self-flagellation. But for the purposes of your money management, it just means reminding yourself that sticking to your budget is what you *want*. Nobody else is forcing you to do it and no one will shame you if you fail. It simply means acting each day in a way that is in your own long-term interests.

Beware of credit cards

There are some financial tools that make the job of sticking to your financial aims even harder than it has to be. Credit cards and other forms of credit – store cards in particular – often lead people into money trouble. Have you ever noticed that it feels less painful to buy a large item using your credit card than using a card that directly debits your current account?

This is because you feel you are gaining goods but not actually parting with money. But your rational mind knows perfectly well you will be parting with the money in a matter of weeks.

For this reason, paying cash is safer if you have a tendency to overspend. You will make a more responsible decision at the point of sale.

If you do choose to use credit cards, make sure you pay off the balance in full by the date specified on your statement. If you do this you should not have any interest to pay, and you will not amass any longer-term debt.

A credit card statement will also name a minimum payment you are required to make. If you fall into the trap of making only this minimum payment, your debt will continue for months or even years, perhaps even doubling over time because of the interest you have to pay.

Debt

On the whole, you will manage your money more effectively by avoiding borrowing. There are exceptions to this, though. The main one is borrowing to buy a home in the form of a mortgage. Few first-time buyers are in a position to be able to pay the tens or hundreds of thousands of pounds it costs to buy a house.

Borrowing is expensive

Many people are simply unaware of the cost of borrowing from credit cards. Some credit cards charge a crippling 29 per cent in annual interest. And rates charged on store cards can be even worse. Some cards issued by women's clothing chains charge 31 per cent in annual interest on outstanding balances on their store cards after the initial interest-free period.

Banks charge between 9 per cent and 20 per cent in annual interest on authorized overdrafts, according to specialist financial information provider *Moneyfacts*. But watch out for unauthorized overdrafts, which can cost as much as 32 per cent.

If you can't pay cash, do you really need to buy it?

Avoiding getting into debt often means making some hard choices. It is tempting, for example, to take out a personal loan to pay for a new kitchen in your home, or to buy a new car on credit.

But if you recognize that your financial health will be better if you avoid unnecessary debt, you must ask yourself if you really need these items. Could you make do, until you can afford to pay cash? Could you buy an eight-year-old car instead? Could you simply repair your current kitchen and brighten it up with paint?

The slow slide into debt

Getting into serious debt is usually a gradual slide. It begins when you decide to buy something you cannot afford. Over time, you might be able to pay off one loan for one item. But if you made one decision to overspend, the chances are that this is part of your general attitude and you will make that decision again.

So the slide into debt is one characterized by steady acceleration. No only are you likely to add to the sum borrowed by additional spending, but interest is charged at the same time.

The only way that spending more than you earn might turn out all right is if your income is set to increase substantially in the near future. Otherwise the problem will only get worse.

Once you have started becoming too indebted, it is easier to ignore the situation than face it because of the hardship that will be necessary to remedy the situation. But obviously the longer you leave it, the worse it will get.

All too often, people do not start to tackle their debts until they have become unmanageable and the options are limited. But tackle them you must if you are ever to get back onto a secure financial footing.

What your options are depend just how bad your debt problem is.

Pay off debts with any savings you have

If you have debts as well as savings, this makes as little sense as actually going out and borrowing money in order to invest it. This is exactly how many people in the City make millions, but for the small investor, this high-risk strategy is unlikely to work.

To understand why it is useless to have debts and savings at the same time, compare the rates (mentioned above) for credit card borrowing with those paid on some high-yielding investments. Top rates for cash ISAs are 5.75 per cent.

Once you've paid off costly credit and store card borrowing, you might be wise to remove temptation and cut up the cards.

And if you do intend to keep using a credit card, switch to one which has a low interest rate. For example, a Visa card from Cahoot – the Internet bank owned by Abbey National – charges just 8 per cent in interest. Read terms and conditions of credit cards carefully, though, as they vary widely.

But what about major borrowings, such as your mortgage? Because mortgages are secured loans, the rate of interest you pay is normally quite low. So paying this off may not be as urgent as some car loans or personal loans. But you could still save interest by using lump sums to pay it off.

If you have equity in your home and are carrying around debts, it might make sense to remortgage and use the additional money borrowed to repay any high-interest debts. By shopping around, you may be able to lower your mortgage rate at the same time. It is a good idea to seek independent advice on remortgaging.

Repay your mortgage early – but carefully

You have to be careful when repaying some of your mortgage, over and above your set monthly repayments. There may be penalties for doing this, especially if you received an incentive, such as 'cashback', when you took the mortgage out. And often the extra capital you repay is only added to your account once a year, which means it will make no difference to the interest charged for many months. So make sure you repay any lump sum at the right time of year.

Don't use emergency savings to repay your mortgage. Once you have used money to reduce your outstanding mortgage, it takes time to get at that money again. You should always keep savings for an emergency easily accessible.

If debt is a problem, seek help

If you are unlucky enough to find yourself with unmanageable debt, there are still plenty of options. It is quite normal that people who have accumulated a large amount of borrowings are unwilling to talk about the problem to other people, and often resist acknowledging it even to themselves.

At worst, serious money problems – particularly if you are the breadwinner of a family – can drive people to suicide. No amount of financial disaster should be paid for with a human life. If you feel trapped by debt, remind yourself that it is a situation you can solve.

Pick the right people to help you

Tell your problem to your local Citizens Advice Bureau or the Consumer Credit Counselling Service, or another independent non-fee-charging money adviser. Your local authority should be able to tell you how to find one.

But avoid fee-charging debt advisers. Their advertisements in the media claim that they can solve your debt problems by structuring your debt so that you only have one low and manageable monthly payment to make. The Consumer Credit Counselling Service says fee-charging firms like this offer no more than the free services available.

Through their advertising, other financial services firms offer you the chance to consolidate all your debts into one secured loan, which will cost you less each month in repayments. A secured loan is similar to a mortgage, in that your property – in practice your home – is held as security against you failing to repay the debt.

Should you refinance your debt?

Secured loans are cheaper than non-secured loans – overdrafts, personal loans, credit card borrowing – because they are less risky for the lender. In many cases they are cheaper to repay each month because the debt is spread over a far longer period than a personal loan.

Although swapping several debts from different sources for one secured loan has its advantages, there are several reasons to avoid this route. It will take you far longer to rid yourself of this loan – possibly 25 years if it is a second mortgage – and over that period you may pay twice as much in interest than if you had chosen a shorter repayment period.

But the real downside of this option is that you are putting your home at risk. Should you get into financial trouble again and be unable to repay this secured loan, you could find yourself homeless with your house being repossessed by the lender.

If you default on a credit card debt or a personal loan, the consequences are serious – you could end up with a county court judgement against you, which will impair your credit record, but at least you will not lose your house.

Once you realize your debt problems are out of hand, the best move is to consult a debt counsellor from one of the organizations above. They may recommend that you negotiate a different repayment schedule with your lenders, for example, rather than taking out a different type of loan.

How do you know when you need help?

When are debt problems serious enough to warrant seeking outside help? After all, most people in this situation are apt to bury their heads in the sand rather than face the depressing truth. Frances Walker of the Consumer Credit Counselling Service says as a rule of thumb if your monthly repayments on debts – excluding your main mortgage – exceed 20 per cent of your net income, then you should get help.

Banks

Most people open their first current account in their teens or at the latest when they go to college or university or get their first job. It is a popular myth that there is some innate benefit in sticking with this original current account – somehow account-holders believe they will build up a good reputation with their bank manager by keeping money in the account and not going overdrawn too often, etc.

There may have been some truth in this one or two generations ago, but times have changed. Contrary to the impression their slick advertising campaigns give, a bank is not your friend. They do not do you favours to reward your loyalty; they are simply money-making businesses that aim to make as much profit as they can.

If you are creditworthy, your bank will gladly lend you money and charge you interest on that. But so will most other money-making institutions.

Defect to a better bank

So there is no reason to keep your current account at one particular bank – shop around to find the cheapest and most appropriate service you can.

Of course, there is one real drawback in switching your current account to another bank, and that is the sheer hassle of the move. It takes some time, and while regular transactions such as direct debits and standing orders are being transferred from your old account to the new, it can be hard to keep track of your money.

But this should be a manageable hiccup as long as you choose a relatively quiet time of your year to make this change – during the summer when workloads are lighter could be a good time for you.

Internet-only banks pay high interest

There are now several Internet-only bank accounts on offer. These tend to offer far better value than traditional branch-based accounts or even accounts operated by telephone and post. Infrastructure costs for these new banks are so low that they can afford to offer not only free banking on their current accounts, but also to pay a competitive rate on interest on credit balances. In some cases, the rates they offer are higher than the returns paid on savings accounts.

Of course to use an Internet bank, you have to have a computer, access to the Internet and feel comfortable with the medium. If you do not have this, there are several telephone-based accounts that offer good value.

How do you choose a good current account? The financial pages of the weekend editions of national newspapers are a good source of up-to-date information on current account deals. Or browse the personal finance magazines on sale at larger newsagents and booksellers (e.g. WH Smith), for a feature on current accounts.

Most current accounts offer a full range of standard features, including cheque books and guarantee cards, debit cards, cash machine cards, standing orders and direct debits. So the choice is based largely on cost and convenience. Compare the rate of interest paid on credit balances, the rates charged on overdrafts and any monthly or annual fees you may be charged whether in credit or debit.

Are premium accounts worth it?

Most of the high-street banks have now started offering what they term 'premium' current accounts. These usually charge a monthly or annual fee, and include a number of services in return. These can range from commission-free foreign currency to discounts on theatre tickets and annual travel insurance.

Generally speaking, it is not worth paying for an account like this. The perks are usually not relevant to you and this is simply a new way that banks have thought up to market fee-charging current accounts. If there is a particular feature you are interested in – say, annual travel insurance – work out how much it would cost you to buy it elsewhere and compare the cost with the account's fee.

You may be exhorted by a bank employee to switch – 'upgrade' – to a 'premium' account, but remember bank staff are salespeople for the institution they work for. While it is in the bank's best interests for you to pay for this type of account, it is probably not in your interest.

Stay aware of your current account balance

If you are to manage your current account well, it is important to be aware of your balance at all times. Obviously, it would be unrealistic to know the amount to the nearest penny, but you should check it often enough to have a fairly accurate idea in your head whenever you write a cheque of how much you will have left after that expenditure.

A tried and tested way of doing this is to use the pages in your cheque book to write down all regular payments, cash machine withdrawals, credits, etc., so that you can tot up your balance after every transaction. However, this is just one extra job to do every time you write a cheque, etc., and you may forget. Also, cheque books are used less today, with debit cards now accepted in most shops.

The most efficient way of keeping track of your current account is to make use of one of the home-accounting software packages on offer. Microsoft *Money* or Intuit's *Quicken* are relatively inexpensive programmes to buy. With the help of one of these programmes, you can input details of all your account activity on a regular basis – say, once a week – and then be able to analyse your spending in detail.

This can be an interesting activity in itself – 'Did I really spend £85 on petrol last month?' – but most importantly it gives you the information to be able to work out realistic budgets for future spending.

Overdrafts

The ability to go overdrawn is one of the useful features of a current account. It gives you the flexibility to be able to cope with unexpected expenses. But overdrafts can also be dangerous if not used carefully.

Avoid going overdrawn without agreeing an overdraft facility first with your bank. If you already have an agreed overdraft limit, try not to exceed that limit without getting permission in advance. The interest charged on unauthorized borrowing is much higher than that for authorized borrowing, and there can also be extra charges involved.

Also, try to pay back any overdraft as quickly as possible, because it is not usually the most cost-effective way of borrowing. If you cannot pay it back within a month, then look at an alternative form of borrowing – a personal loan, perhaps. Apart from the cost of maintaining an overdraft, being constantly in debit rather than credit makes it hard to see how much you are currently spending.

If your money matters are veiled in confusion, overspending is far more likely, and your debt can snowball.

Current account mortgages

Many current accounts are now linked to mortgages. This system has one great advantage – any credit balance you have in your current account is offset on a daily basis against your mortgage borrowing, thus reducing the interest charged on your home loan.

This can save you thousands of pounds in the long term, and is a suitable method of borrowing for some. But if you find keeping track of your current account at all difficult, steer clear of this type of product. It will only make you more confused about how much money you are actually free to spend. And the less in control of your money you feel, the more likely you are to make poor judgements about what you can or cannot afford.

Insurance

Before you start saving money for your future, you need to consider whether you need any insurance and if so which types. There is no point in building up a raft of savings and investments without first making sure your most basic needs would be taken care of if the worst happens.

Would you have enough to live on if you were unable to work? Would your dependants survive financially if you died, and would they be able to keep the house?

With insurance, it is important to realize that you cannot cover every eventuality. Overwhelmed by all the potential disasters they could insure against, many people don't take out any insurance at all.

It is unpleasant to think about dying, but surely worse to imagine dependants left poverty-stricken and homeless as well as grieving. If you have a mortgage on your home, you probably took out a life insurance policy, which is designed to provide enough money to pay off the loan if you die prematurely. If not, or if the policy has lapsed, it is vital that you take a suitable one out.

As well as making sure the mortgage would be paid, you may need additional life insurance to provide a lump sum or income as well. Check to see what financial protection you already have. If you belong to your employer's pension scheme, there may already be certain benefits which would be paid to your dependants in the case of your death. Otherwise you can buy insurance with the same benefits elsewhere.

Different types of life insurance

Life insurance comes in many shapes and forms. Term assurance covers you for a fixed period, while whole-of-life assurance continues to cover you until you die. Premiums can be either guaranteed or subject to change throughout the period the policy is in force.

Before buying life insurance, you have to work out exactly what your needs are and how they might change. It is best to discuss it with an independent financial adviser.

- *Term assurance* guarantees to pay out a sum of money if the person insured dies within a given time. There is no investment element – at the end of the term, the contract ends and nothing further is payable on either side.
- *Whole-of-life assurance* will pay the amount assured on your death, whenever it happens.
- *Level term assurance* is term assurance where the amount paid out if you die remains unchanged throughout the term.
- *Decreasing term assurance* is generally the cheapest form of term assurance. The amount paid out on death decreases as the term goes on, making this cover useful for those with repayment mortgages.
- *Convertible term assurance* gives you the option to convert the policy to a whole-of-life policy in the future. The benefit is that you cannot be turned down for whole-of-life assurance whatever your state of health.
- *Renewable term assurance* is similar to convertible term assurance, except that you have the option to exchange the original insurance for another term assurance contract at the end of the term.
- *Increasing term assurance* provides for the sum insured to rise each year by a fixed percentage, enabling you to keep pace with inflation.

If your family would need an income, a cheap way of providing cover for this is to buy family income benefit insurance. This is a type of term assurance which pays out a regular income, rather than a lump sum which they would then have to invest.

Life insurance premiums have fallen

In principle, life insurance premiums become more expensive the older you are. So if you bought a policy at age 30, it is worth hanging onto for the term.

However, life insurance premiums have actually fallen quite significantly since the early 1990s. People buying life insurance in 2001 paid, in many cases, half as much as someone taking out the same protection policy just five years before.

Life insurers across the board have been cutting rates because of increased competition in the market, and a view that people will live longer than the insurers had previously thought.

Why? The AIDS scare in the 1980s is the main factor. Insurers thought at the time that the scale of the epidemic would be much worse than it turned out to be – at least in the UK.

Also, heart conditions and cancers are leading to death less frequently than they were. And trends towards healthier lifestyles, advances in medical technology and better sanitation are all helping us as a population to live longer.

So if you have had a policy for more than five years, it could be worth shopping around to see if you can cut your monthly premiums. Rates vary widely from insurer to insurer.

It is not that one or two insurers are good value across the board – different life companies are cheaper for different age groups. They try to target different types of customer.

But if you do decide to switch life insurer, watch out for possible pitfalls. Look carefully to see what type of term assurance you have. If it is pure term assurance, it is relatively simple to compare it with a new contract. But if you have renewable or convertible term assurance and your health has deteriorated since you took it out, a new contract may now be far more expensive. You could even be uninsurable now.

Do not cancel your old policy until you have the new one in force.

Insuring against ill health

As insurance companies never tire of telling us, one in four men and one in five women will suffer a serious illness before retirement. If this left you unable to work, would you have any income at all?

As long as you are permanently employed and have been with the same company for a while, it may well be that your employer would continue to pay you for six months if you became ill and unable to work. For the six months following that, you would probably receive half pay, and then you would be on your own.

But there is no minimum standard for employers to adhere to, so you must find out what your employer's policy is.

There are two main types of insurance to protect against serious illness: critical illness insurance, which pays out a lump sum if you are diagnosed with a life-threatening illness; and permanent health insurance (PHI), which provides you with an income if you are unable to work for a long period (not to be confused with private medical insurance, which covers hospital and medical costs).

Of the two types, financial advisers tend to agree permanent health insurance – also known as income replacement insurance – is the more affordable and useful option. Even if you don't have any dependants, permanent health insurance is worth having. Few of us would like to end up not only incapacitated but also reliant on paltry state benefits. (Refer to pages 105–8, Chapter 5, income protection insurance.)

Don't let insurance salespeople scare you

One thing to remember about insurance is that the people who sell it usually exploit your fears to do it. What if your house burned down? What if you had a stroke? You can't insure against everything, and have to make your own decisions about which misfortunes you do want or need to protect yourself financially against.

Don't let a salesman frighten you into buying a policy without having the chance to think about all the issues calmly on your own.

Car

Though a car is not nearly as large an asset as your home, it is still a big expense, and one that continues throughout your life.

Buying a car

You may be offered a company car. Although it may seem a good perk of your job, think carefully before accepting it. Many employers now offer cash alternatives to their staff instead of a company car, because they are so heavily taxed. (Refer to pages 91–2, Chapter 4 on company car taxation.)

If you buy your own car, the main options are to use a private leasing agreement, to make a financing deal to purchase a new car, to buy a new car outright or to choose a second-hand car.

Do careful research before buying a car to make sure you are getting the best deal. Good car magazines are useful sources of information and should help you decide between the relative merits of buying new or second-hand.

Shopping around for car insurance

Car insurance premiums have been rising fast since the end of the 1990s. Insurers have faced a huge increase in the cost of claims over the last few years, and the industry as a whole has been making a loss on the car cover business. Part of the reason claims have been more expensive for the insurers has been the trend towards increased litigation.

But the car insurance market is still very competitive, and by shopping around drivers can save hundreds of pounds on the annual cost of their car insurance.

The most obvious way to shop around is to phone a number of insurers, get a quote from each and then compare them. But this is a time-consuming process as giving your details to just one insurer over the phone can take around 20 minutes.

And don't expect it to go smoothly. While connected to one insurer you are likely to be passed from one department to another and probably find yourself having to repeat tiresome personal details to another call operator.

You can buy car insurance on the Internet, though at the moment, this is likely to be another frustrating experience. Waiting for each page of an application form to download leaves you tapping your fingers and should your trusty PC freeze before you have finished, you may feel like hurling it out of the nearest window.

Drivers using 'quick quote' services offered by some car insurers on the Internet have sometimes found that when they go through the long version of the application the premium is much higher. Others invite you to fill in an application online, but when you want to take out that insurance you have to repeat the information to a real person or even put it in writing.

So save your nerves by limiting your selection to two or three insurance providers that you are confident should offer a good deal. One of them could be a broker, such as Swinton or Peoples' Choice, which will search a number of companies to get you the best quote.

Is it best to use a broker?

Brokers say they can give competitive quotes for a wider variety of people than a direct insurer. This is because they place a risk with a range of insurers, each of whom specializes in one particular type of risk – safe drivers, those with convictions, driving older cars, etc.

Direct insurers, on the other hand, say they can offer better value insurance because they do not have to pay commission to brokers. But of course they have increased advertising and marketing expenses. Take your pick.

When it comes to making a claim, there are advantages in having bought a policy through a broker. A broker has a duty of care to their client – the insured – to ensure they get good service from an underwriter, and a broker can use its bulk-buying muscle to make sure clients are dealt with fairly when they claim.

Ways to keep your premiums low

Apart from shopping around to get the lowest price for your cover, there are plenty of ways you can help yourself to keep the cost of your car insurance to a minimum.

If you park your car in a locked garage each night, or at least off the road and on a driveway, this can keep premiums down. Keeping your mileage within limits can also save money, with many insurers charging lower premiums for insurance if the car is driven less than 10 000 miles a year.

You can opt to pay a higher excess on each claim. With one insurer, for example, volunteering to pay the first £100 of each claim instead of the more standard £50 would have saved around £30 a year in premiums.

And consider the cost of insurance before you actually buy a car. This is particularly important for men in their twenties. Faster cars attract much higher premiums, especially for men under 25. Don't let too many people drive your car. Your car insurance will increase dramatically if you put your teenage children on your policy.

Proving to insurance companies that you are a better risk for them also encourages them to offer you cheaper cover. You can do this by completing a Passplus driving course. The scheme has been running since 1995 and involves a course of six driving lessons with an approved driving instructor. The course covers driving on motorways, on rural roads, in different weather conditions and night driving.

Drivers successfully completing the course earn a certificate issued by the Driving Standards Agency. Sixty per cent of motor insurers support the scheme, giving drivers with the Passplus certificate a discount on their premium. The discount should be equivalent to one step of progress on a no-claims discount – and this can make premiums 20 per cent cheaper.

Home

Once you decide to leave your parents' home, you need a home of your own. Whether you choose a flat or a house, the options open to you are to buy or to rent.

Buying a home as soon as you can reasonably afford it makes sense, given the history of rising property prices in the UK over the last half-century. Since they have tended to rise faster than the increase in average earnings – and at times much faster – the later you climb onto the property ladder the more difficult it will be.

Buying a house is a big commitment

However, buying a home is a serious commitment and one that you may not be able to get out of easily or quickly. It takes time to sell a house or flat. Even in the most buoyant of property markets, you would be lucky if the transaction went through within four months. But if the market is slow or in decline, it could prove impossible to sell quickly.

Many people in the 1990s found themselves stuck for years in the same property, because they had 'negative equity'. This meant they had bought their house or flat in the late 1980s when property prices were rising fast, but when they wanted to sell in the 1990s, the price had fallen below the price they paid. For people with mortgages of 80 per cent or even 100 per cent of the value of the property, they could not afford to sell, because they simply wouldn't get enough money to pay off the mortgage.

This is not likely to happen so dramatically in the near future, but nothing is certain. So don't buy a house or flat if it would be a disaster to be stuck there for a few years.

Renting is more flexible

When you rent a home, you lack security, but you do have flexibility. But since paying rent is usually more expensive than making the repayments on a mortgage for a similar property, as soon as you are in a position to buy a home, this is a good option.

Saving up as much as you can to put down a deposit is the best way to start. While 100 per cent mortgages are available, the terms on them are not nearly as good as for those where you pay for more of the house yourself. This is because if you have a deposit of, say, a quarter of the value of the home you want to buy, then the risk for the lender that it will get its money back if it has to repossess the property is less.

How much will a mortgage lender give you?

Before you start looking in estate agents' windows, you need to know how much you can afford to spend. Apart from your deposit, how much can you borrow?

Lenders will usually give you a mortgage of up to three times your annual gross salary. If you are a couple, they might only lend two and a half times your joint salaries. But they will take other things into account, such as whether you owe any money.

Don't automatically borrow as much as a bank is willing to lend you. It is much more important to work out how much you can comfortably afford to pay every month. And if you are a couple who may have children in the future, make sure you will be able to meet the payments on just one salary.

There are hundreds of different types of mortgage on the market, and it is important to choose the right one for you. You can save yourself the bother of comparing products from several different providers by using a mortgage broker to find a good value home loan for you.

But even if you do this, you still need to know the different types of loan on offer.

Repayment mortgages

The first choice you face is the repayment method – apart from the interest the lender charges, how will you pay back the capital sum you borrow? The options are: repayment mortgage or interest-only mortgage linked to an investment vehicle.

With a repayment mortgage, you pay back the amount you have borrowed gradually, by paying each month a mixture of interest on the loan and capital – which is the sum of money you borrowed at the start. It is the easiest type of mortgage to understand.

At the beginning of the term – usually 25 years – nearly all of your set monthly repayment is interest and only a small part of it is capital. But after a few years, when you have repaid a significant proportion of the loan, the interest gets less, allowing you to repay the capital faster. The last payments are nearly all capital and very little interest.

The advantages of a repayment mortgage are that they are easy to understand, they are safer because there is no investment risk involved and you are free to shorten the mortgage term by making extra capital repayments.

Interest-only mortgages

An interest-only mortgage is one where all you pay the lender each month is the interest on the loan. Your loan remains the same until the end of the 25-year term. With an interest-only mortgage you nearly always pay some money each month into a savings scheme. The idea is that after 25 years, the savings scheme will have enough money in it to repay the whole loan you took out.

This savings scheme could be an endowment policy, an ISA or a personal pension plan. An interest-only mortgage is hardly ever called that – it is usually named by the savings scheme you use to pay it back, such as an endowment mortgage or a pension mortgage.

The main advantage of an interest-only mortgage with some kind of investment is that you may be lucky and end up with more than you need to repay your loan. But, on the other hand, the investment might not do so well, leaving you with less than you need.

Having chosen your repayment method, you then need to decide what type of interest rate you want. The main options are fixed or variable rates.

Variable rates

With a variable interest rate, the rate of interest you pay follows bank base rates – it all depends where the Bank of England decides to set them.

Fixed rates

If you opt for a fixed-rate mortgage, your rate is static for a period, which could be anything up to 25 years. The advantage is that you know where you stand, and will be able to budget for your monthly mortgage payments in advance. The disadvantage is that interest rates may fall below your fixed rate, but you will still have to carry on paying at the higher rate.

Also, if you take on a particularly low fixed-rate mortgage – which is basically a discounted, fixed rate – your lender might make you stay with that lender even after the period of fixed rates has finished. If you don't, there could be stiff penalties to pay (see 'Being tied to your mortgage lender').

Capped rates

A capped interest rate is one where the lender guarantees the rate will not go above a certain level. But if base rates fall, you will benefit from this.

Discounted rates

You could choose a mortgage with a discounted interest rate. This is variable rate, but to entice borrowers, the lender reduces the rate for a period of time. This is an incentive, and there may be certain conditions attached to it. You will probably be tied to the lender for the period of the discounted rates and possibly even after that phase has finished.

Being tied to your mortgage lender

Watch out for tie-ins, or mortgages that carry early redemption penalties, when you choose a loan. Although it seems fair enough for a lender to require you to stick with its deal until that particular deal finishes, if you are tied in after that, you have to put up with whatever level of interest rate it charges. At that time there could be far more competitive mortgages on the market, and you should leave yourself free to take advantage of them.

Flexible mortgages

A new breed of flexible mortgage has sprung up in the last few years. They take many shapes and forms, but the principle is that you can pay more off your mortgage if and when you want, and you can also take a break from payments for a few months if you need to without getting into trouble.

They can take the pressure off, if for instance you lose your job for some reason, you won't immediately have to worry about losing your home too.

The current account mortgage is one type of flexible mortgage. It basically combines your current account, savings account and mortgage in one account. Although your overall balance can look horrifying – £85,000 in the red? – there are some real advantages of this way of banking. Interest on the debt is calculated daily, and at any one time your credit balances cancel out part of your debt. This means you incur less interest, and so are theoretically able to pay your debt off earlier.

Also, because instead of earning interest on your savings you are simply saving yourself mortgage interest, the benefit to you is gross rather than net of tax. So it is like receiving interest without paying tax on it.

Choosing an independent financial adviser

Finding a good independent financial adviser (IFA) will save you the time it takes to research which of the many financial products on the market is best for you. IFAs have the resources and expertise to know which products are around and are legally required to recommend the most suitable product for you. You may be able to sue them if they give you bad advice.

But there are several different types of financial adviser. Some are independent but others are not. They may be tied agents, representing a bank or insurer, and therefore able to sell you products only from that company.

IFAs can offer you a product from any company. They should have professional qualifications and be authorized by the Personal Investment Authority (PIA) or Financial Services Authority (FSA).

If you need a complete review of your financial circumstances including tax and legal matters, financial planners are the best option. Solicitors and accountants can also be authorized to give financial advice.

How IFAs earn their money differs. They either earn a flat fee from you or get commission on the products they sell. Discuss payment soon after you make contact. If you are working on a fee-only basis, you may be able to agree a complete fee in advance.

It is easy to think advice you get on a commission basis is free. This is not the case. You are still paying for it out of the financial product you buy. Ask how much commission will be paid and if you feel this is too much, you could agree a fee instead.

IFAs now often rebate commission, and discount brokers routinely rebate commission back into the product you are buying. But check to see whether they offer advice as well, and whether you pay for this.

According to Consumers' Association research, the best advice is given by fee-charging financial advisers. Some people prefer to pay fees so the adviser is not tempted to sell you an unnecessary product. After all, the best advice could be to do nothing.

Chapter 3

Building Up a Pension

Do I need a pension?

Unless you know for a fact that you will die before you stop working, you need to build up a private pension to live on in retirement. Gone are the days when the state provided enough for everyone to have a decent standard of living in retirement – if those days ever existed in the first place. Slowly but surely the welfare state's coverage is being rolled back in response to the changing shape of the Western world's population.

Health in general has improved in the UK and other developed countries, and at the same time the number of babies being born has fallen. So people are now living longer and there are fewer working people per pensioner in society. This trend is expected to continue for some time yet.

Financially this means that if the welfare state continues to operate with the same principles it has had in the past, there will be an ever greater burden placed on the shoulders of those who are young and in work.

So we are now being encouraged by our government – or forced, depending on your viewpoint – to save enough money during our working lives to provide us with a pension.

Most people in higher-income brackets have long saved for their own pension, as the state pension was never going to be nearly enough to give them the quality of retirement they wanted.

So should I take out a pension plan?

There are many different financial products on the market to use to prepare financially for retirement. Pension plans are the most obvious ones. But before looking at the products, it makes sense to assess exactly what it is you are trying to achieve.

Inevitably, you will be aiming to create an income for yourself in retirement. You may also want to build up some capital as well, as this is more flexible. Capital is useful for larger outlays you may face once you are retired such as holidays, cars, house repairs and lump sum gifts to children. And capital can always be turned into extra income if you need it.

How much money do I need to put away?

The big question is how much money you want to have in retirement. When you are only in your thirties this is a difficult question. But start by looking at your current lifestyle and project it as realistically as possible into the future.

How do you imagine your lifestyle in retirement will differ from your current life? Perhaps you have children now. Once they are adult they will no longer live with you. You will be spared the daily expense of feeding, clothing and housing them. You may be able to live in a smaller house.

Will you live where you do now? Perhaps you now live in a city because of work, but once this phase of life finishes you will move to a smaller town or even the country. This may be less expensive in a number of ways.

If you have a mortgage to repay now, this will probably be repaid by the time you retire. This alone will leave you hundreds of pounds better off each month. You may run two cars now, but only need one when you finish working.

However, not everything will be cheaper in retirement. Since your day will no longer be filled with work, you are bound to take up other pastimes. If reading and walking are to be your main activities, you won't face huge costs. But you may travel more frequently and for longer. With more free time, entertainment may cost much more than it does at the moment.

Can I really predict how much money I will need?

When you are planning to invest for retirement, it is worth building up a picture of exactly what it is you are saving for. At the very least, this will help you focus on retirement as a realistic prospect rather than a distant future which may not really happen. This will help you to take retirement planning more seriously.

As a guide to the amount an average person would be content to live on in retirement, good occupational pension schemes aim to provide scheme members with a pension equal to two-thirds of the salary they are on just before retirement.

But even if you are able to build up a realistic picture of what your expenditure might be in retirement, there are several other wild cards that are more difficult to predict. You cannot know the future level of annuity rates in 30 years' time, nor can you tell what rate inflation will run at in the meantime or how strong investment growth will be.

Financial advisers say that in practice most people start making serious financial plans for retirement when they are in their mid-thirties or early forties.

Typically, at this point they estimate that they will need a monthly income in retirement of between £1,500 and £2,000. But they can only afford to contribute about £200 a month into a pension. At today's generally expected levels of growth and inflation, these contributions would only be adequate to produce pension income of about half their target.

Save as much as you can spare now

In practice you need to work out how much you can afford to invest in a pension or other retirement-oriented investments and be content to tailor your retirement spending to the income you end up with at the time.

Pension advisers can give you an estimate of how much you should ideally have to live on in retirement. But we are all individuals and it is worth considering the future realistically, given your own set of circumstances.

Assessing the pension assets you already have

If you have been working for a decade or more, you may have already built up some pension assets by contributing to occupational pension schemes. If you left the company and therefore stopped making payments to the scheme, then the assets you have are known as frozen or preserved pension assets. They may be in an occupational scheme or a group personal pension.

Before creating a serious plan for pension savings, you need to get a good picture of the provision you have already made.

It is usually relatively easy to write to the trustees of the pension scheme and request a projection of your pension benefits.

Do you have a long-lost pension?

If you do have frozen pension assets, it is vital to keep in touch with the trustees of those schemes, notifying them of any changes of address. All too often private pension benefits are left unclaimed. Employees often build up pension entitlements at their place of work, but contact is lost when they leave the job.

The Pension Schemes Registry has details of 200 000 pension schemes. Every year, it has between 40 000 and 50 000 requests for help in tracing lost pension benefits.

How do people lose their pension benefits? Some people believe that because an employer has gone out of business, the pension scheme is no longer viable. But pension schemes are run independently by trustees, so they are sheltered from a bankruptcy. Employees who leave are often reluctant to have anything to do with that employer again, so they fail to inform the company pension scheme administrators of their current address.

It is not clear how many pension assets remain unclaimed, but estimates have put the figure at anything between £10 billion and £77 billion.

If you think you may have lost track of a pension you once contributed to, contact the Registrar of Pensions, PO Box 1NN, Newcastle-upon-Tyne NE99 1NN.

Should you transfer frozen pensions into a new plan?

If you do have frozen assets from more than one pension scheme, it can be complicated to keep track of them all. It would be neater to have all these assets under the umbrella of one pension plan.

Technically it should be possible to transfer these funds into one scheme. But it is extremely difficult to know whether or not this is a wise move.

Transferring pension assets from one scheme to another often carries relatively high costs. Also – particularly with occupational pension schemes on a final salary basis – you may end up missing out on subsequent benefits which cannot be predicted at the time of transfer. Some corporate schemes, for example, find they are very well funded and give their pensioners large annual pension increases as a result.

You need a good pensions adviser to work out whether a pensions transfer is worth it, but even then, the adviser may not be able to predict certain future advantages of remaining in the scheme.

Different types of pension plan

There are many different types of pension plan. The main differentiation is between occupational pension schemes – one offered by your boss – or a personal pension plan.

Occupational pension schemes and stakeholder pensions

If you are employed and lucky enough to have access to an occupational pension scheme, then that is nearly always the best option, advisers say. If you join the scheme, your employer makes a contribution on top of the money you pay in. Some schemes are non-contributory, which means you don't have to put in any money yourself.

As with personal pensions and stakeholder pensions, you get tax relief on your contributions. This means if you are a higher-rate taxpayer, for every £60 you contribute, the Inland Revenue adds another £40. For basic rate taxpayers, the Inland Revenue pays in £22 for every £78 of contributions. When you draw an income from your pension fund, this is taxed, but it is unlikely at that point to be at the higher rate. (For more on occupational pensions, refer to pages 76–82, Chapter 4.)

Until 2001, workplace pensions have only been offered by larger employers. But from October 2001, nearly all companies have been required by law to have a stakeholder pension scheme to offer employees. However, in these cases, the employer is not yet required to make a contribution on behalf of the employee.

But if you are self-employed, or your employer does not offer a pension scheme, a personal pension plan is the obvious option.

Personal pension plans

Personal pension plans are investment schemes run by fund managers, insurance companies, banks or building societies, and designed to provide you with an income in retirement.

At your chosen retirement age, which can be anything from 50 to 75, you use your pension fund to buy an annuity – an annual income for life. You can choose to take up to 25 per cent of the fund as a tax-free lump sum.

You can take a personal pension out whether you are employed or self-employed; though if your employer offers a pension scheme, that is usually the best option.

The Inland Revenue gives you tax relief on your contributions and there are limits on how much you can contribute to a personal pension. Up to age 35 you can put in 17.5 per cent of your net earnings, and this proportion rises in stages to a maximum of 40 per cent for those over age 61.

There are many different types of personal pension on offer, and it is worth shopping around or consulting a good independent adviser. Pension companies charge for setting up and administering plans, and for transferring the pension to another provider, and these costs should be compared. Some plans are far more flexible and cheaper than others. (Refer to pages 109–12, Chapter 5 on personal pensions.)

Stakeholder pensions

Stakeholder pensions were introduced in April 2001 by the Government. They are low-cost, basic, personal pension plans which meet certain government guidelines for good value and flexibility. They must allow a regular monthly contribution of as little as £20 per month, carry an annual management charge of no more than 1 per cent, and 100 per cent of contributions must be invested.

Unlike personal pensions, stakeholder pensions can be used by non-earners, such as full-time parents, as well as those with an income.

Though the costs are low for stakeholder pensions compared with some personal pension plans, this does not mean they are necessarily the better choice. There are now about 31 providers offering stakeholder pension products, and the same number selling non-stakeholder personal pensions, according to financial data provider, *Moneyfacts*.

Financial advisers say that, though the costs with stakeholder pensions are very reasonable, costs shouldn't be looked at in isolation. There is no benefit in paying just 1 per cent in annual management charges if the performance of the actual pension fund is so poor your return is less than 6 per cent.

A non-stakeholder pension may have the advantage of offering a wider variety of investment funds, possibly with higher potential returns. Better and more complicated funds are more expensive to run.

Look at the charges on pension plans

Deciding which of the many pension plans on the market is the best for you can be complicated. Advisers say the main things to look at are: the charges levied by the pension provider, how flexible the pension contract is and how well the underlying investments are likely to perform. Probably the best way through the pensions maze is to take good independent pensions advice.

But it is now relatively easy to compare pension products, particularly over the Internet, which means if your affairs are fairly simple, professional advice may not be necessary. With the advent of stakeholder pensions, many of the old insurance companies have made their personal pensions more user-friendly, giving them more transparent fee structures.

The snag with all pension schemes is that you cannot access the money you've paid in until you retire. This could be as early as age 50, however. When you do get your hands on the money, a quarter of the pension pot that has built up can be taken as a tax-free lump sum, but the rest must ultimately be used to buy an annuity – an income for life.

Make a careful choice

Taking out a personal pension plan is a huge financial decision. With hundreds of plans on the market, probably the best way through the pensions maze is to take good independent pensions advice. But you do have to pay for it. Advisers may charge a fee of between £250 and £500 for setting a personal pension up depending on how complicated it is.

To guide consumers through the complicated issue of pensions, when stakeholder pensions were introduced the Government developed decision trees, which are given to applicants by stakeholder pension providers. These are flow charts that help consumers make a choice on which pension to buy without having to pay for advice.

Not surprisingly, they have been criticized by financial advisers. They say the decision trees oversimplify the decision on which pension to take out; not taking advice could be very costly in the end.

You can use other investments to save for retirement

Pensions, however, are not the only way to save for retirement. It is wise to save money outside a pension plan as well, because there are fewer restrictions on when you access that money and how you can use it.

You could opt to use other tax-efficient savings vehicles – personal equity plans (PEPs) and individual savings accounts (ISAs) – instead of pensions.

The discipline of pension plans can be useful

Some people don't like being tied up with pensions legislation and losing control over their capital, but for others, the externally imposed discipline of pensions is very helpful indeed. If you think you are at risk of plundering your pension pot before you reach retirement, then the iron rules of a personal pension could be invaluable.

Pensions advisers say that particularly for the young – those in their twenties – the discipline of a pension plan is useful. It is much more likely at this age that you will be tempted to dip into another more accessible investment you might have made, which was intended to be kept for retirement.

No matter how good our intentions are when we start saving for a pension, it is important to choose a method that will impose some discipline to save us from the occasional hijackings of our spendthrift alter egos.

Regular contributions are best

Apart from choosing a pension plan where contributions once made are locked away, it is also a good idea to commit to making regular contributions by monthly direct debit. Though pensions and other investments can also be built up by making annual single premiums, in practice there may well be a reason why you decide to miss that annual premium when the time comes around.

When you are older – in your mid-thirties or later – the prospect of retirement will seem more concrete, and you can more safely use other investments to save to fund your post-career life.

Building up a pension in your thirties and forties is simply a matter of accumulating a pot of money that can be used to fund retirement. The fact that you are going to use that money to produce an income is irrelevant in the decades during which you are still working.

Other investments

This lump sum can be built up using another investment vehicle – preferably one that is tax-efficient, such as an ISA (refer to page 137, Chapter 7).

For many people who have larger sums to invest, venture capital trusts (VCTs) are a good, tax-efficient way of building up a retirement nest egg.

Venture capital trusts

Investing through a VCT is a way of sharing in the growth of smaller companies, while leaving the decisions to the experts. VCTs are quoted investment trusts – collective investments run by managers who invest in the shares of smaller companies. Some of those firms may be existing or early-stage companies while others are management buyouts.

Probably the main reason for anyone to invest in a VCT is the huge tax breaks these investment vehicles offer. If you have a large capital gain from the sale of assets, including business assets, you can defer paying tax on the proceeds by investing it in a VCT. Up to £40 000 of tax can be deferred in this way.

This tax deferral is only available if you are investing at the initial subscription of a VCT, and the investment must be made within 12 months of selling the taxable assets.

Apart from the tax deferral opportunity, with a VCT you get tax relief at 20 per cent on your original investment, but again, only if you invest at the start. This means someone investing £10 000 will receive £2000 in tax relief. But you must hold the shares for at least five years to qualify for that, otherwise the relief is clawed back.

There is no income tax payable on dividends paid by VCTs, and no capital gains tax on VCT profits. And the VCT itself pays no capital gains tax when it sells stakes.

The most you can invest in a VCT for tax purposes in any tax year is £100 000, which can be spread across more than one VCT.

Investors can buy shares in VCTs directly from the manager of the trust, or through a stockbroker. There are usually several VCTs on offer at any one time, but investment groups tend to open VCTs for new subscriptions around the end of one tax year and the beginning of the next.

Investing in new companies with little or no track record is risky, and VCTs are high-risk investments. But the broad spread of investments held in a VCT lessens the risk.

The pros and cons of releasing equity in your home

In retirement many people find themselves property-rich but relatively cash-poor. They may be the proud owners of a substantial house and be unwilling to trade down to a smaller property for many reasons. Perhaps they still have many visits from children and grandchildren. Or they may have lived in the same house for so long that they are reluctant to give it up for sentimental reasons.

Some financial services companies offer products which make it possible to create an income from the capital in your home, without actually having to move.

Equity release schemes come in many shapes and forms, but the idea is basically the same. You sign over part or all of the value of your home to a company in exchange for a lump sum or an income for life, and a cast-iron guarantee that you will have the right to live in your home for the rest of your life.

However, from a financial point of view, the best solution is to sell your home and buy a cheaper one; then use the profit to produce an income. But although that is the best option it is not always practical.

Most plans are either sale-based or mortgage-based. Under sale-based plans, or home reversion plans, the homeowner sells all or some of their property in return for a life tenancy, usually for a token rent, plus a lump sum or an annuity or both. Providers include Stalwart Assurance; Home and Capital Trust; and Carlyle Life Assurance.

Home income plans are mortgage-based, with a fixed-interest mortgage used to buy an annuity for a fixed income for life. Other mortgage-based schemes include a simple interest-only mortgage, which is repayable on death or when the property is sold. Some products roll up the interest and this is simply added to the amount owed.

How much income can an equity release scheme generate? For a single man of 75, a home income plan based on a £30 000 mortgage with an annuity might produce a net annual income of £1309.20, according to Hinton and Wild. A home reversion scheme involving the sale of 50 per cent of a house worth £200 000 would generate a lump sum of £53 452. This lump sum could then be invested to produce an income.

Equity release schemes got a bad name in the late 1980s, with bad schemes leading to disaster for some elderly people. House prices were buoyant and large mortgages were raised. The plans combined these mortgages with investments, often in high-yield bonds. But when interest rates shot up and investments performed badly, the investment return was not even enough to cover the mortgage payments, let alone provide an income as well, so some pensioners faced losing their homes.

Today's products are less risky. Most providers of home income plans participate in Safe Home Income Plans (SHIP) or at least adhere to its code of practice. SHIP is a company formed in 1991 to protect planholders from 1980s-style fiascos. Under the code, members pledge to, among other things, provide fair and complete presentation of their plans and make sure the legal work is performed by a solicitor of the client's choice.

If you propose to use a home income plan, it is essential to get good independent advice before doing do. There is a big difference in the value offered by the different products on the market, and some schemes can be irreversible in practical terms.

You should make sure you will still have the right to move house in the future. Find out if you will have security of tenure for life, and who benefits from any appreciation in the value of the house. Ask what would happen if house prices were to fall? Would you or your heirs end up with negative equity?

Becoming a landlord

The increased popularity of buy-to-let mortgages, which allow you to borrow money to buy a house that you then rent out, indicates that many people are using property to generate income in retirement.

More than a million people now own a second property, with two-thirds of those rented out. Buy-to-let mortgages put second homes within the reach of ordinary people, because the rental income covers the cost of the mortgage repayments.

Pension advisers say it is a good idea to consider property as an investment alongside conventional pension plans. This is an investment which already produces an income, so does not need reinvesting when you actually come to retire.

But watch out for the practical difficulties of being a landlord. In practice, landlords say that expenses are often higher than originally anticipated. If you have a change of tenants once a year, you can expect to end up forgoing rental income for at least one month every year. This alone can throw your calculations off balance, and cut your profit margin to the bone, or worse.

Buy-to-let schemes really come into their own where the landlord sees considerable capital growth. For example, if you bought a property in west London in the mid-1990s, you could expect to have seen the value of your asset double by now. But many people who bought in less popular areas in the late 1980s are still saddled with negative equity.

And property in this form is not a very liquid investment. If you decide to sell, it could take months, and if you need to get at the money at a time when the housing market is depressed, you could end up having to take a loss.

Pensions and divorce

If you get divorced or your marriage is annulled, when the financial settlement is being negotiated, pay attention to the pension assets that have been built up during the marriage.

Courts now have to take account of the value of your pension rights. If you are a woman who has spent many years bringing up children and have not been in paid work or were only working part-time, then you will have missed out on many years of contributing to a private pension.

Your spouse, on the other hand, may have been contributing consistently over that period. If the marriage remained intact, naturally this would not be a problem because your joint finances would support you both.

New legislation brought in at the end of 2000 allows that pension to be legally split into two separate pension contracts. Under provisions in the Welfare Reform and Pensions Act, which took effect on 1 December 2000, a non-earning spouse can now claim a share of the breadwinner's pension nest egg.

The law applies to personal, occupational and State Earnings Related Pensions Schemes (SERPS). Pensions can be shared for divorce petitions commenced on or after 1 December 2000. Before this new law, there were other ways of taking account of a pension fund as a matrimonial asset in a divorce, and these methods can still be used.

Cash or property could be taken in lieu of pension rights or part of the pension could be 'earmarked' or 'attached'. By earmarking part of the pension, a proportion of the eventual income would be paid to the claimant's spouse in retirement.

But the main problems with earmarking were that it left the claimant with no control over the pension. If the spouse with the pension were to die after starting to draw the pension, then the income would cease. And the pension holder could retire as late as he wanted, leaving the ex-wife with no income in the meantime. Also, pension rights would be lost altogether if the non-earner remarried.

Pension-sharing is very useful in that it means a divorc-ing couple can achieve a clean break financially. The spouse claiming a share of the pension fund – or claimant – should take independent financial advice on how to deal with the financial asset, because there are many implications in this decision.

It is not a good solution for everyone. Transferring pension funds from one scheme to another can be expensive. Actuaries and solicitors have suggested the administrative cost could be around £1200.

If the pension fund is only worth £5000 or less, then splitting it would not be worth it. It would make more sense for the spouse without the fund to take some other matrimonial asset in lieu. Pension-sharing is expected to be most appropriate for couples within ten years of retirement with substantial pension assets.

Chapter 4

Employee Benefits

Of course for most employees, a salary is the main reward from their boss. But particularly for people working in large organizations, there are many other perks offered, which can add up to a substantial value.

Profit-sharing and share ownership schemes can sometimes completely outweigh any salary you take, particularly if you have a top position at an investment bank. Until early 2000, staff working for Internet-related businesses were often content to take options on the shares in their companies rather than extra salary. In retrospect, however, this usually turned out to be a bad mistake, because the financial fortunes of many Internet companies and their share prices have plummeted.

Some companies are now starting to offer flexible employee benefits packages rather than automatically providing all employees with a range of benefits, some of which may be of little or no use to them. Employers' consultants predict that this more targeted method of rewarding and protecting employees will prove far more popular for both staff and their bosses in the future.

Employees are generally offered an overall level of benefit. They can choose, for example, to take a greater proportion of it in private health insurance and less as a company car.

Pensions

When you get your first job, the whole subject of pensions is incredibly dull. At that age, retirement is still decades away, and it is very hard to relate to the needs you will face in the distant future.

But statistics show that the vast majority of us will fortunately reach retirement by not dying before the age of 60. And given that people are healthier than ever, on average men can expect to spend a decade on this earth after they have finished working while women can expect to have 15 years in retirement.

As mentioned in Chapter 3, we will increasingly have to rely on private financial arrangements to fund our retirement rather than income from the state.

Membership of a workplace pension scheme is a major job perk. Whatever your age, before you decide whether to accept or reject a job offer, take the pension scheme offered into account.

The main benefit of an occupational pension scheme is that unlike a personal pension – virtually the only option for the self-employed – your employer tops up your own regular contributions. In some cases, your boss matches your payments and in others they even make all your contributions for you. In good schemes this can mean that you are effectively paid an extra few hundred pounds a month – albeit in delayed salary.

The pensions mis-selling scandal of the 1990s highlights just how good a deal occupational pension schemes really are compared with personal pension plans. From 1988 to 1994, seduced by high levels of commission, many financial advisers wrongly advised their clients to leave occupational pension schemes, or not to join in the first place, and to sign up for personal plans instead. But the upshot was that thousands of people were worse off. The slow process of recovering compensation from the advisers is still going on.

But while it is now generally agreed that occupational pensions are a good thing for employees, this does not mean you should go into one blindly. You will probably make substantial contributions to the scheme too and, as with any financial product, you should make sure you know exactly what it is that you are buying before you sign on the dotted line.

You should ask some questions before you commit yourself. Find out what type of scheme it is and what your benefits are.

Some workplace schemes are in fact group personal pensions. This is really just a personal pension plan of the type you could buy separately as an individual, and should not be thought of as a company scheme. The benefits compared to the contributions are not likely to be as good as with a real occupational scheme. Get advice from a good pensions adviser on the merits of joining.

However, a group personal pension may well offer a better deal than a personal pension plan. Your employer may be making contributions too, and the charges could be lower than for a personal pension plan because of the economy of scale.

There are the two basic types of occupational scheme: money purchase or final salary. Most pensions experts agree that final salary schemes are usually the best for the employee, and they are still the most common. About 90 per cent of UK employees in occupational pension schemes are in final salary schemes.

Final salary schemes

With a final salary scheme, the amount of income you get when you retire is a proportion of your earnings at or near retirement. For each year you are in the plan you receive a guaranteed amount of pension.

Money purchase schemes

With a money purchase scheme, contributions from you and your employer are invested. When you retire, the fund that has built up is used to buy a pension income or annuity. Unlike final salary schemes, there are no guarantees – the income you end up with depends on how the investment performs.

How much do you have to contribute?

Find out if you as well as your employer have to make a contribution. You usually do, although there are some non-contributory company pension schemes where only the employer contributes. Public sector pension schemes tend to be non-contributory, although some would argue salaries are lower to take account of this perk.

Even if you are not making contributions to the scheme yourself, look closely at the product. You could be lulled into thinking that your pension needs are being taken care of but then find out only too late that your employer's contributions were far too small to build up much of a retirement nest egg at all.

For contributory pensions, employee contributions are typically set at around 5 per cent of earnings. You may have the option of contributing at a lower level – say 3 per cent – or at a higher level which could be 6 per cent. At the lower level the benefits would obviously be less than at the higher.

Tax relief on your pension contributions

Contributions made into either an occupational or personal pension plan attract tax relief. This means the Inland Revenue rebates the income tax you have paid on the money you put into your pension. The effect of this is that if you pay tax at the basic rate of 22 per cent, the Revenue will add an extra 22 pence for every 78 pence you pay into your pension. If you earn more than about £34 000 a year and therefore pay income tax at the higher rate of 40 per cent, the tax relief is even more substantial.

Because of the tax relief available, there are legal limits on how much you can pay into a pension. The law allows you to pay up to 15 per cent of your salary into an occupational pension scheme, so there is usually room for you to increase your contributions if you want to.

It might be wise to do this if, for instance, you joined a company pension scheme fairly late in your working life. You would risk retiring on an inadequate pension if you made no more than standard contributions.

And with a money purchase scheme, you need to check regularly to see if your pension fund is on target to reach the amount you need. If not, you may have to step up your contributions.

Topping up your pension

By law, a company must offer you a scheme whereby you can make extra payments into your pension. Extra contributions can be made through an additional voluntary contribution or AVC policy, which is a top-up pension. In most cases, you pay in regular amounts, which are invested and form a fund to buy extra pension benefits at retirement.

Employees in a final salary scheme may be able to buy what are known as 'added years', entitling them to the same retirement benefits as members who have been in the scheme for longer.

The AVC policy sponsored by your company is likely to have very low charges, or one that has no charges at all. Though this is likely to be the best value way of topping up your pension, it is not the only option.

You could choose to pay into a free-standing AVC policy. This is run by an insurance company, is likely to have higher charges, but has the advantage of being more flexible. It may also offer you access to different investments which you believe will result in higher growth rates. But financial advisers warn people to be wary of free-standing AVCs, as the company's AVC policy will invariably be more cost-effective.

What if you leave the company?

What happens to your pension if you leave the company while you are still in the pension scheme? This depends how long you have been in the scheme. If you leave it after less than two years' membership, your only option will probably be to have your contributions refunded.

Pension schemes are unwilling to shoulder the cost of administering very small frozen or preserved pensions. The refund you get does not include the tax relief your contributions attracted, nor will it include your employer's contribution. There may also be charges from the scheme administrators for establishing the plan.

But if you have been in the scheme for longer than this, you can transfer the pension that has accumulated to another pension scheme – it may be another company scheme or a personal pension. Or you can leave the money where it is, making the pension 'paid up'. What you are left with may also be referred to as frozen or preserved pension. You can still join another pension scheme in the meantime.

You may be able to transfer your benefits from one company scheme to another on a like-for-like basis, meaning your guaranteed benefits under the new scheme reflect the years you worked for your old employer.

In a paid-up pension scheme, final salary benefits left in place will usually rise each year with inflation up to 5 per cent. Where the scheme was a money purchase scheme, the money you and your employer put in will remain invested in the fund ready for you when you retire.

How much will the scheme pay you in retirement?

It is important to have some idea how much your workplace pension will pay you when you retire. If you are in a final salary scheme, this depends on the level your pay has reached by the time you retire, and the number of years you remain actively in the scheme. The scheme may aim to pay you a pension equal to half or two-thirds of your final salary after you have worked for the same employer for 30 to 40 years.

In a money purchase scheme, on the other hand, your employer may give you an estimate of what your pension fund value will be at retirement. This is only a guide and hopefully a conservative one. The sum you will really end up with depends on how investments perform in the meantime, so the estimate would usually give you two figures. One figure might assume 6 per cent growth and the other 12 per cent.

This projection of what your pension fund will be worth means little unless you take account of inflation. The better pension schemes will give you an indication of what your funds might be, based on a real growth above inflation of between 1 and 5 per cent a year.

It is this pension fund that you will use to buy an annuity, or pension income, when you retire. Annuity rates fluctuate, so the level of annual income you will retire on depends on annuity rates at that time.

For final salary schemes, the benefits are guaranteed. This is why this type of scheme is gradually dying out – companies would prefer their employees to shoulder the risk of the stock market.

With money purchase schemes, you should know where your money is being invested. You may be given a choice of investment funds for your money. If this is the case, your scheme advisers will hopefully recommend the right fund for your particular circumstances.

How to invest your pension fund

Investment experts typically advise employees who have at least 10 to 15 years left until they retire to have their pension fund invested in a medium-risk fund consisting of stocks and shares. When they get closer to retirement, they would be advised to switch their money to a safer but slower growing fund of government bonds or insurance company with-profit bonds.

To save you having to bother with the investment side of your company pension, many money purchase schemes offer what is known as a *lifestyle option*. If you choose this option, then your pension fund is automatically moved to different types of investments at particular ages, based on the thinking outlined in the paragraph above. If in doubt, it is worth consulting an independent financial adviser on how to invest your pension.

There are likely to be other benefits linked to your occupational pension scheme. These may include life assurance and/or sickness insurance. Private medical insurance may also be available to pension scheme members, though you do have to pay tax on this benefit.

Occupational pension schemes must allow you to take a proportion of your pension as a lump sum on retirement rather than as income. But the actual proportion allowed depends on when you joined the scheme.

With money purchase schemes this may be up to 25 per cent of the pension fund. A final salary scheme may give you the option of exchanging income for a cash sum at the rate of, for example, £8 of cash for every £1 of pension income you give up.

Your pension scheme is not simply for your personal benefit. Your spouse or other dependants will probably be entitled to a widow's pension if you die first, and if the scheme incorporates a death-in-service benefit, they will benefit from that if you die before retirement. A spouse's pension may not be more than two-thirds of the pension you would have received.

But find out from the administrators of your pension scheme exactly who counts as a dependant in your company pension scheme. Older schemes sometimes stipulate that only the named spouse may benefit. But otherwise you may be able to nominate your partner, even if you are not married. Whether a partner of the same sex may benefit depends on the pension scheme.

Some public sector pension schemes will pay benefits to a member's legal spouse only at the date of death, while certain private sector schemes will pay out a dependant's pension to a whole range of people.

SERPS

SERPS, as mentioned before, stands for the State Earnings Related Pension Scheme. When you come to retire, SERPS is paid on top of your basic state retirement pension.

The Government has said it plans to reform SERPS in 2002, with a new vehicle – the State Second Pension – providing a more generous additional state pension for those on low or moderate incomes and others.

When you retire, you can take benefits from an occupational pension as well as the basic state retirement pension and SERPS. But you can decide to contract out of SERPS during your working life. This means you and your employer pay lower National Insurance contributions and the money is instead redirected into your occupational pension scheme. Most people in occupational pensions are contracted out of SERPS.

Life insurance

As already mentioned, many companies give their employees free life insurance which is known as death-in-service benefit. In many cases, this benefit is part of the occupational pension scheme. But it is also usually available to employees who have not been with the company long enough to be eligible to join the pension scheme. Death-in-service benefit pays out to your next of kin on your death either a fixed sum, or a multiple of your gross annual salary at the time of death – typically two or three times your annual salary.

Life insurance that is offered by your employer has a major advantage. If you are considered by life insurers to be high risk – say, you are a woman whose mother died early from breast cancer – then you will find life insurance quotes very high. Sometimes you may even be considered uninsurable.

But this type of individual medical assessment is not required for life insurance offered through your employer. This is because the underwriter views the risk in terms of a group of lives – all the employees who are covered – rather than you as an individual. So insurance that might otherwise be unaffordable is feasible as an employee.

Health insurance

Many companies offer private health insurance as a perk. Two of the biggest providers of this financial cover are BUPA and PPP. As long as you do not have to contribute to the private health insurance you are offered at work, then it is probably worth accepting it.

However, private health insurance is a taxable benefit, so it will never be completely free. If you feel it is of no use to you at all, then decline the offer.

It is often the case that an employer will pay the full cost of private health insurance for the employee, and cover will be available for the rest of the family as long as all or some of the cost of this is borne by the employee.

But you should read through the insurance policy carefully to be aware of exactly how you are covered. The benefits available from private health insurance vary widely, and if this free cover does not protect you against some risk which you consider important – say, dental costs – then you need to be able to take out your own cover as well.

If you are required to make a contribution to the private health insurance offered through your employer, think carefully whether it is worth it.

Share-ownership schemes

Nearly all of the largest companies in the country operate some form of employee share plan. Of course the idea is to make staff feel more responsible for the overall success of their company and cultivate an interest in its share price rising. Undoubtedly, share-ownership schemes at work do have this effect. But they are also great job perks, which can reap huge rewards for the participants of these schemes.

Don't rely on the money just yet

However, be warned that share prices can be extremely volatile. Just as they can show huge returns, so they can also go down sharply. Never rely on money you hope to get from a share-ownership or share-option scheme at work, until the shares are sold and the cash is sitting in your bank account.

All too often share-option owners optimistically behave as if the money they hope to receive is already in the bank. In some cases they raise a larger mortgage than they can reasonably afford, confident that they will be able to repay a chunk of it a few months after taking it out once they are able to exercise their share options.

But all it takes is a drop in general stock market confidence and the company shares could lose a quarter of their value – or worse. If something specific to your company rattles the market – perhaps profits have been overestimated six months before by a gung-ho finance director – you could easily see 75 per cent of the share value erased.

Even the shares of major UK companies can take an unexpectedly sharp dive. Shares in BT, for example, horrified employees who held them when they lost two-thirds of their value in 18 months. They fell from £13 in January 2000 to £4.60 in July 2001.

And shares in once-rock-solid UK retailer Marks and Spencer were worth just £2.62 in July 2001, down from £4.25 in September 1999.

How share-option schemes work

Share-ownership schemes usually take the form of savings plans that last for five years. You contribute a monthly sum, and are probably given a range of possible contribution levels.

At the start of the plan, you are given a share-option certificate – a document which gives you the right to buy shares in your company on or after a specific date at a specific price and using the money you have built up in the scheme. The money you pay in is held in an interest-bearing account.

The price stated on the share option document – the exercise price – is typically about 20 per cent lower than the current share price. But the hope is that when you come to exercise the options in five years' time the shares to which you are entitled will have risen substantially in price, and perhaps be worth twice the amount you will pay for them.

This means that when you exercise the share options, you buy the shares at such a favourable price that you could make an instant profit by selling the shares.

Should you keep the shares or sell?

If you are keen to keep your investment risk as low as possible, selling the shares immediately is probably your best option. You may like the idea of owning shares in the company you work for, but from a purely financial point of view it makes little sense and is in fact a very risky thing to do unless you already own shares in several other companies.

To make money out of the stock market you need to have a diversified portfolio. This means you should hold shares in several different companies – ideally at least 10. And those companies should be spread across a broad range of industries, so that if profits in the telecommunications sector, for example, take a dive, your shares in electricity suppliers will at least remain steady.

However, there is an advantage in holding onto shares in your company. Because you actually work there, whether your job is in the post room or on the board of directors, you are likely to get a feel for how well the company is doing. You may notice if orders for the company's goods start to weaken or, on the other hand, if the mood of your bosses is consistently buoyant.

As long as you feel confident that your company is remaining profitable and growing, the chances are that the shares will be valued by the stock market, and their price will therefore flourish.

So to keep your risks within limits, but also to keep yourself in a position to benefit from the rising fortunes of your company, you could choose to sell half of the shares you acquire and use the proceeds to buy units in a diversified unit trust, while retaining the other half of your shareholding as it is. (Refer to pages 141–2 in Chapter 7 on spreading your investment risk.)

Different types of share-ownership schemes

There are several different types of share-ownership scheme for employees. The differences between them are mainly to do with the way the capital gains you make from the scheme are taxed. When you are deciding whether or not to take advantage of the share-ownership scheme offered by your employer, it is not very important to know exactly what type it is. After all you will only be offered one type.

These share-ownership schemes are nearly always worth taking advantage of. The shares are priced so favourably, or the option price so low, that your company is practically giving its shares away.

And if the worst came to the worst, and over the five-year period the company's share price were to fall sharply from the price on the option, you could decide not to buy them. Instead you could take the money out of the scheme, and the sum you saved would still have attracted interest over that period.

A new type of share-ownership scheme for employees was introduced in July 2000, called All Employee Share Ownership Plan (AESOP). Less than one-tenth of companies have one in operation at the moment, according to research by consultancy Watson Wyatt.

At the moment most large companies have schemes in the form of savings-related and approved company share-option schemes.

AESOPs have a number of advantages over other types of scheme, including flexibility of design, the ability to be implemented alongside a company's existing share schemes and tax efficiency. Employers' consultants expect AESOPs to become the most widespread method for employers to deliver shares to staff.

Usage of approved profit-sharing schemes will continue to decline up until the removal of associated tax benefits at the end of 2002. No new approved profit-sharing scheme could be introduced after 6 April 2001.

Company cars

Cars may look like four-wheeled vehicles to someone from outer space, but we earthlings know better. They are status symbols of the highest order and this is why, for many, a company car is the most decisive perk a potential new employer can offer.

But company car schemes are now on the decline. This is because tax on company cars is now so high that employees often find it cheaper to run their own cars.

Company cars are assessed by the Inland Revenue as a benefit in kind, meaning that up to 35 per cent of the list price of the car is treated as annual salary. So, since most people who earn enough to justify this perk are higher-rate taxpayers, company car drivers can find themselves paying 40 per cent tax on a third of the value of a car each year.

Now, more than half of companies that offer company cars to staff also offer a cash alternative. In many cases employers have linked up with car-leasing companies to help employees arrange their own private leasing contracts.

Tax rules based on emissions

The new tax rules on company cars take effect in April 2002. At this point, company vehicles will be taxed on the basis of their carbon dioxide emissions.

The new rules will make tax lower for drivers of cars with carbon dioxide emissions at a lower level than 165 grams per kilometre, who also drive fewer than 2500 business miles a year. But the losers will be those who drive cars with high carbon dioxide emissions, and who do high annual business mileage.

Exactly how you will be taxed on a certain company car depends on a host of factors. The Inland Revenue's web site is a good source of information on this subject, and a special section guides you through the process of finding out how much extra tax you would be liable to pay if you took on a certain company car.

If you are offered a company car, make your own careful calculations and try to resist it if your tax bill would increase enormously.

Chapter 5

Self-employment

For people in many professions, becoming self-employed is part of their natural career progression. The only way they can move forward is by working for themselves.

Journalists and writers, for example, can often progress only by going freelance. Their other option is to keep working for a publication and move up the management hierarchy – a path that distances them increasingly from the actual business of writing.

Within the last decade it has grown common for computer programmers and other IT workers to become self-employed, working as contractors to companies rather than employees of them. Apart from small business owners, there are members of many other occupations that usually involve being self-employed, such as doctors, shop owners and barristers.

Working for yourself puts you in control

For the sake of freedom alone, people from almost every walk of life may at some point in life decide to set up their own business, rather than work for someone else's firm.

The biggest advantage of self-employment is the control it gives you over your life. It is up to you when and how you work. Office politics become dramas of the past. But there are also big risks to shoulder. If you fail to get work, then obviously you will earn nothing, and you could even be stuck with debts if you have had to borrow money to set up your business in the first place.

However, employment is now rarely really secure. In many ways, a freelancer or consultant who has more than three clients is in a more secure position than an employed individual. Hardly anyone is immune from possible redundancy. Even civil servants can face redundancy resulting from cutbacks in public spending.

On the other hand, the likelihood that a freelancer would lose all of their clients in one go is slim.

From a financial point of view, self-employment should in theory pay you more effectively for the work you do, as long as you are good at your job. As a rule, self-employment is a great separator – the competent tend to do better than they would as employed individuals, while the less competent fare worse than they would if employed.

Tax

Dealing with tax often seems a daunting issue for the newly self-employed. But unless you have a business which has employees, it is actually relatively simple.

An accountant can help you with your books and file your tax return for you, but you will be more in control if you learn to do it yourself.

You must keep business accounts for five years if you are self-employed, and you are effectively required by the Inland Revenue to do so. Remember to keep comprehensive records of all business expenses so that they can be written off against tax.

Although dealing with your own tax and National Insurance may seem a big responsibility and complicated at first, there are many tax advantages to being self-employed.

If you work for yourself, you can claim more allowable expenses than employees. These expenses all add up and can be offset against tax, which means your taxable income will be correspondingly smaller.

Also, unlike employees, tax is not deducted from the earnings of the self-employed before they are paid. They are taxed under the rules for Schedule D Case I or Case II. Employees are taxed under Schedule E.

Tax bills must be paid on time, and once you are established as self-employed for tax purposes you will be asked to make payments on account. This is usually two payments a year – one before the end of January and one before the end of July – which together equate roughly to the amount of tax payable for the previous tax year.

But tax is generally payable months or even more than a year after the income has been generated. This gives you the opportunity to put that money to work in the meantime.

A good habit to get into is putting aside a certain percentage of all gross earned income to cover tax and National Insurance. Provided you are likely to fall into the basic rate tax bracket – earning £33 000 or less in one tax year – then putting aside a quarter of gross earned income should cover your subsequent tax bill.

However, once you have two years' experience of how much tax you actually end up paying after expenses, etc., you will be able to get a more realistic idea of how much you need to put aside. It may be as little as a fifth.

The money you put aside for tax is best kept in an easily accessible savings account, paying as high a rate of interest as possible. The interest you can earn on your tax money is substantial.

For example, if you earned £28 000 during the year and gradually put a quarter of this away in an account paying 5.5 per cent in interest, you could earn around £500 in interest on the money before you had to pay it to the Inland Revenue.

Write off your expenses against tax

There are many allowable business expenses for tax purposes. If you work from home, then you can claim for a proportion of the household bills which relate to your workspace.

Other allowable expenses include:

- all your administrative costs such as phone bills and stationery;
- the cost of trade and professional journals;
- travel costs related to your business and hotel accommodation costs;
- interest on bank and other loans that relate to your business;
- repairs and maintenance to business equipment;
- motor expenses if your car is used for work, such as AA membership, petrol or diesel and parking charges.

Keep up with accounting and invoicing

If you are self-employed, you need to be very organized about the financial side of your business. When you are busy working for clients to keep the money coming in, it is often tempting to leave your own paperwork and accounts, promising yourself you will catch up at the weekend.

But the longer you leave jobs like invoicing and checking that you have been paid for work you have done, the more likely it becomes that you will miss out on payment for one of your jobs in one way or another. Being haphazard about paying in cheques you receive in the post can obviously lead to disaster.

For most self-employed people, the routine that works best is to set aside one afternoon a week for administrative jobs including accounts. If your business brings in enough revenue, consider using a bookkeeper.

Do you need an accountant? Unfortunately only an accountant can tell you this! Try to find an accountant who comes recommended by someone you trust. Arrange an initial meeting with them, and they should be able to tell you if they will be able to save you any tax and how much their fees would be. It may be that you are already well aware of how to minimize your tax bill and the fees could not justify the simple convenience of having an accountant prepare your tax return for you.

IR35

Many self-employed people are now affected by a new rule from the Inland Revenue called IR35. The new rule means that many self-employed people with limited companies are deemed to be in 'disguised employment'. Because of this, their typical tax and National Insurance liability could rise to 35 per cent – the level paid by employees – from about 21 per cent before.

IR35 applies to any individual with a limited company, especially if they work for one or very few clients. If you are in this position, you should consult an accountant to find out how you are affected. (Refer to page 161, resources section, Institute of Chartered Accountants in England and Wales.)

Mortgages

Getting a mortgage as a self-employed person has its problems. Nearly one in five of the UK workforce now works on a self-employed or temporary basis, but many mainstream mortgage lenders are still as reluctant as ever to lend to those with a fluctuating income unless you have solid proof of past earnings.

It is very hard to get a mortgage unless you have three years' accounts to show. And many lenders insist that these accounts be certified by an accountant. Providing accounts can be a problem, particularly for someone who has become self-employed in the last two years as earnings are likely to have been low.

The accounts often provide an inaccurate picture of what level of mortgage the would-be borrower can actually afford. Many expenses can be written off against tax, effectively shrinking the business' profits and therefore the amount a lender will grant.

Banks tend to see the self-employed as a riskier proposition, but for many people, becoming self-employed marks a phase of higher income.

Status and self-certification loans

There are usually two options open to self-employed people looking for a mortgage. Either you go for what is known as a status loan, which could be for up to 100 per cent loan to value, and give two to three years' audited accounts or tax statements.

Or you can put up a large deposit yourself, and borrow 75 per cent or less loan to value. In this case, you can take the self-certification route, which means you do not have to give proof of income. The usual credit checks are carried out, and these may include a current or previous lender's reference and a bank reference.

So if you work for yourself, the easiest way to get a mortgage is to put up at least a quarter of the property price yourself. Regardless of the lender's faith in your ability to repay the loan, it then has the reassurance that it would – unless house prices fall by more than 25 per cent – be able to get its money back by selling the house. This also cuts out the need for a costly mortgage indemnity guarantee, or MIG, which covers the lender against any shortfall if the property is repossessed.

It is essential you choose the right lender. Nationwide's subsidiary, UCB Homeloans; the Mortgage Business; and Bank of Scotland are three lenders that specialize in self-certification mortgages. Some lend as much as 85 per cent of property value without demanding proof of income.

First port of call should be your own bank. If you use a bank for business, then you probably have more of a relationship with them than the average customer. The bank would not need to carry out all the credit checks as it would already know your history.

Flexible mortgages suit the self-employed

Flexible mortgages, which allow borrowers to overpay at times and underpay at others, can be particularly suitable for the self-employed (refer to page 48, Chapter 2).

Using a mortgage broker or independent financial adviser will save you a lot of legwork, and usually cost you nothing. An IFA would simply take a procurement fee from the lender, as well as commission on any insurance product sold.

Insurance

Apart from the obvious financial security of a regular pay cheque, employees are cushioned against many other financial risks. They may be members of an occupational pension scheme, and this may include life insurance. They may also be provided with private medical cover by their company.

As well as this, most employers continue to pay their staff when they are ill. In the civil service, for example, it is normal to receive full pay for the first six months of sickness and half pay for a further six months.

But self-employed people have none of these financial benefits. On the one hand, if you work for yourself you can decide whether you need this degree of financial protection, but on the other hand, if you do want it, you have to pay for it yourself.

How much protection do you need?

If you are single and have no dependants, then life insurance is simply not necessary. Ask yourself whether anyone would be in trouble financially as a result of your death. Although it is an unpleasant scenario to conjure up in your mind, try to work out what the financial implications would be for your dependants.

For example, if you have a partner who works, and you share in caring for your children, then if you died your partner would have to spend more on childcare. On the other hand, if your partner became the childrens' sole surviving parent, it might be better if they could spend more time with the children to give them the extra attention they would probably need – at least for a year or two. This would mean your partner would need more financial assistance to make up for loss of all or a portion of their salary. Try to add up how much this would all cost – either as a lump sum or as an ongoing monthly amount – and then attempt to insure for this sum.

If you work it out as a monthly income for your dependants, then you have to estimate how much capital they would need to produce that income. You can do this by assuming an annual investment return of 5 per cent. All you need to do is multiply the figure for required monthly income by 20.

If you use 5 per cent as the assumed investment return, this takes account of the effects of inflation during a period when your dependants would be drawing an income from the capital sum, because a return of 5 per cent is low enough to allow the capital to be invested in financial instruments that would produce some capital growth as well as income – a fund which included some shares, for example.

If you are self-employed and have no dependants, even though life insurance is of no use to you, critical illness cover may be helpful. Critical illness insurance pays out a lump sum upon diagnosis of any of a range of serious illnesses, such as a heart attack or cancer.

For those without dependants, this can be a useful type of insurance to have. If you become seriously ill, not only may you be unable to work, but you may face additional expenses, such as help with cleaning and cooking at home.

Private medical insurance may be worth having if it is paid for by your employer, but it is rarely considered a necessity. Just over six million people in the UK are now covered by private medical insurance, but the majority of PMI policies are sold as job perks. BUPA says 60 per cent of people covered by its medical insurance are covered through company schemes.

Of those who buy it personally, PMI really appeals to private business people. Often those who run their own business and cannot afford to spend time being on a hospital waiting list.

The market for PMI is very broad, with over 25 different providers in the UK offering around 450 different plans. Traditional medical insurers BUPA and PPP have in recent years been joined by general insurance companies such as Norwich Union and Allied Dunbar.

PMI premiums are generally rising by more than inflation. The main reason is simply that people are making more claims on their insurance. Also, technology in hospitals is increasingly expensive and this keeps PMI costs soaring. There is now more eligible treatment that can be done, with cancers very much more treatable now.

Choosing which PMI policy to buy can be a minefield. Ideally, you should use an insurance broker who specializes in this area. Contact any independent financial adviser who should be able to direct you to a specialist broker if they are not able to do it.

Levels of cover

The policies on offer vary widely in the level of cover they provide. Most costly are the deluxe plans that include dental, optical and maternity care and alternative therapy. Next come the comprehensive plans which offer full refunds for most services including outpatient treatment and private ambulance service. Budget plans at the other end of the scale often do not cover outpatient care or are only subject to certain conditions.

Especially when opting for a budget policy, make sure the hospitals you would want to use are included. And remember to contact your insurer before having treatment to ensure that any costs incurred will be covered.

Take care when applying for PMI that you are scrupulously honest about your medical history, IFAs say. If there is a family history of something, you should mention it, because the chances are very much higher that is you will need special cover for it.

Income protection insurance

Probably the most useful financial protection for self-employed people is income protection insurance (IPI). Confusingly, this type of cover is also known as permanent health insurance. There are other names for it as well – it can be called anything from long-term disability insurance to income replacement insurance; from disability income insurance to personal disability insurance.

With income protection insurance, for a monthly premium, the insurance company will pay you a monthly income if you are unable to work through ill health. Financially, long-term illness can be a bigger disaster than death. You are unable to work, but still have ongoing expenses.

According to the Consumers' Association, every year nearly two million people are off work for more than six months through illness or injury – this is 20 times the number of people who die before they are 65.

If you are self-employed, the state pays you very little if you are too sick to work. You are entitled to incapacity benefit at £62.20 a week, rising to £69.75 a week after a year off work. If you were under 35 when you became unable to work, from the second year you are off work you receive an extra £14.65 a week, while if you were under 45, you would be given an extra £7.35.

It is very important, if you work for yourself, to work out how you would manage financially if you were unable to work for a long time. It may be that family members can be relied upon to help, and savings might go a long way. But otherwise, private insurance is the answer.

Major providers of IPI include Norwich Union, Permanent Insurance and Friends Provident.

It is worth using a good intermediary when buying IPI. This market is more sensitive than life cover, advisers say. Some policies contain exclusions for pre-existing conditions, for example, and an IFA or broker can make sure you know exactly what you are buying.

An IPI policy will only ever pay out a certain proportion of your income – usually up to 65 per cent. This is laid down by insurers, because it is in their interests to give you an incentive to return to work.

Income protection policies are written for a certain number of years with a given deferment period. The deferment period is the number of weeks you have to be off work before the policy starts paying out. If you choose a longer deferment, then the premiums will be cheaper. You can also keep your monthly premiums down by opting to be covered only until the age of 60 rather than 65, if you are confident that your savings could tide you over those five years before retirement.

For self-employed people, the most common deferment period is 12 weeks, while those in employment generally choose 26 weeks. Some providers offer policies that will pay out on the first day or first week of incapacity, but these are far more expensive.

As mentioned, not all policies define inability to work in the same way. It is important to choose one that will pay out if you cannot do your own occupation. Some pay out only if you are unable to do any job at all, while others tread a middle path by paying if your health prevents you from doing any 'suited' occupation.

Depending on the policy you opt for, the premiums may be guaranteed throughout the term or reviewable. Premiums on reviewable policies will not increase simply because you make a claim or are older, but providers may alter premiums if their level of claims on the whole changes significantly.

While life insurance is cheaper for women than for men, because statistically they live longer, IPI is about 50 per cent more expensive for women than for men.

So premiums depend on your sex and age, but also on the type of job you do. If your occupation is considered to be a dangerous one – scaffolder, for example – the premiums are likely to be higher than if you were a desk-bound clerical worker. And the medical examination you may have to have is usually more stringent than for life insurance.

The ABI (Association of British Insurers) points out that you should check with the person who sells you the insurance whether you will need to tell your insurer if you change occupation – or even if your duties change within the same job.

Pensions

A major drawback of self-employment is that you don't have access to an occupational pension scheme. With a workplace pension, your contributions are boosted by payments made by your company which, in the end, obviously means a lot more pension for your money.

Also, self-employed people – unlike the employed – do not receive SERPS in addition to the basic state pension. SERPS stands for State Earnings Related Pension Scheme, and pays an extra sum in retirement. As the name suggests, contributions depend on earnings, as do benefits.

So those who work for themselves need to put more into their private pension to compensate for the lack of SERPS benefits. Pensions advisers suggest that broadly speaking, self-employed people should be putting 10 per cent of their net relevant earnings away into a personal pension plan or equivalent retirement savings.

However, earnings are rarely consistent for self-employed people. Income fluctuates from month to month, and from year to year. The best policy, rather than committing to make regular monthly contributions to a pension plan, is to make single annual contributions, once you know how much you have earned in one tax year. In this way you will be able to put more away for retirement in good years and less in the leaner periods.

Some small business owners mistakenly believe they do not need to save money for retirement because they can simply sell their firm when they stop work. They hold the vague hope that the proceeds of this business sale will fund an income for the rest of their lives. Their business is their pension, they say.

But pension advisers warn against taking this attitude. It is extremely risky because there is no way of knowing whether a business will be worth anything at all when you come to retire. That date may be 20 years in the future, and who can predict which businesses will still be competitive then? The economic conditions may have changed beyond recognition by that time.

And apart from the risk that the business will no longer attract buyers, many businesses – such as accountancy firms – are only worth anything at all because of the expertise of their staff. So once you have retired, your asset may not have much to offer anyway.

What is a personal pension plan?

A personal pension plan is a financial product that allows you to make regular savings for your retirement. Sold by insurance companies, banks, investment companies and building societies, personal pension plans invest the money you pay in.

You have to pay charges to the pension scheme provider, but on the other hand you get tax relief on your contributions. This effectively means that the Inland Revenue tops up your contributions by the same amount that you pay as income tax. For example, for every £78 a basic rate taxpayer pays in, £22 is added by the Inland Revenue.

When you take out a personal pension, it is vital to consider the level of fee that the pension provider levies. For many people, it is simply too complicated and obscure to find this out and this is why pension providers have for many years been able to get away with – in some cases – extraordinarily high charges.

Research from the Consumers' Association has shown that if you choose a personal pension that carries high charges, the pension you end up with could be half the amount you would have had with a better value plan.

Apart from the cost of the product, you should also consider how flexible the plan is. Income for the self-employed is rarely without its peaks and troughs, and if you run into a longer-term lull in terms of work, you will appreciate the ability to halt your pension contributions for a while without being heavily penalized with extra charges.

Even if you are employed, this flexibility is very important in today's employment climate where jobs are no longer for life. A flexible personal pension will also allow you to vary the level of contribution made.

Anyone thinking about starting a personal pension must be clear that this is a very long-term investment, pensions advisers say. You should not put money into a pension unless you are sure you won't need it. Once your money is invested in your personal pension, you cannot get at it until you are at least 50.

Even traditional pension plans have a certain degree of flexibility. You can choose to take the pension at any age between 50 and 75, without necessarily retiring. A quarter of the sum that has built up can be taken as a tax-free lump sum, and it is up to you which type of annuity you buy. This might be one that rises each year or one where the monthly income remains static.

You do not have to pay contributions monthly. They can be paid annually once you have worked out how much you can really afford.

Banks and insurance or investment companies offer personal pension plans, and there are quite a few different types around.

- *Unit-linked plans* – this is the most common type. At retirement, the size of the fund your premiums have grown to is linked to the investment performance of a stock market fund.
- *With-profits plans* – these are less risky than unit-linked plans. They are insurance policies where you also share in the profits of the insurer by means of bonuses. These bonuses cannot be taken away once added.
- *Unitized with-profits plan* – a cross between unit-linked and with-profits.
- *Unit/investment trust plans* – your contributions are invested in unit trusts or investment trusts (two different types of investment fund), and the lump sum you end up with at retirement depends on the performance of the trust. These tend to have low charges and are often very flexible.

Stakeholder pensions were introduced by the Government in 2001 and in many ways, this new format of retirement plan has simplified things.

It is very important to get good professional advice before you commit yourself to a pension scheme. (Refer to pages 48–50, Chapter 2 on choosing an IFA.)

Because of the tax break you get on contributions to a personal pension, the Inland Revenue limits the amount you can put into a plan. This depends on your age and is a percentage of your net earnings. Only net earnings below £95 400 are counted – at least for the 2001/2002 tax year – so this sets a maximum limit on the contribution possible in any one year.

How much can you contribute to a personal pension plan?

Age on April 6	% of your net earnings
Up to 35	17.5
36 to 45	20
46 to 50	25
51 to 55	30
56 to 60	35
61 to 74	40

Setting your own salary

It is important if you work for yourself to set financial goals. To a large extent this is determined by your outgoings. If you already have many financial commitments – perhaps you have children and a mortgage – then you need to earn a minimum amount to keep your head above water.

You need to work out how much your time and skills are worth. Though there may be set rates paid in your line of work, it is likely that there are more or less lucrative options within that.

Setting financial and earnings goals will also help you keep a limit on the amount of your time you spend working. Unless you are a workaholic, you will appreciate your free time. You may find that you are able to achieve your financial goals by working for five hours a day.

Chapter **6**

Working Abroad

The world is shrinking. Not literally, of course, but in economic and trade terms, barriers have come down. The world's major companies are increasingly global – they are beginning to operate in terms of industrial sectors rather than geographical regions.

This is particularly the case in the pharmaceuticals, information technology and telecommunications industries. What this means for individuals is that there are many opportunities within a single company to work in different countries.

Within the European Union, workers have for many years been free to find employment in different member states, making the whole area a single job market.

Why work in another country?

There are plenty of reasons why you might choose to work outside the UK – either temporarily or for the rest of your career. You may fall in love with another country, or one of its inhabitants. Perhaps the standard of living or the climate of another country appeals to you, or taking a foreign assignment will help you up the career ladder. Maybe you just want a new experience.

You can take the independent route and look for a job in your chosen country with a local employer, as long as you can overcome the language barriers. But the reality is that many people in the UK who work abroad are employed by a UK company with interests abroad.

Negotiate a good package before you go

There are many additional costs faced by expatriates that you must take into account before agreeing to work abroad. Whether you are applying for a foreign post with a UK-registered company or are being sent abroad by your current UK employer, it is essential to make sure your financial package is good enough.

It has been widely reported that the days of generous tax-free expatriate packages are over. Large companies with international operations now see that there is value in recruiting local expertise. And even though staff from headquarters are still often needed to transfer skills to locals, these companies are well aware that setting the foreign staff apart by boosting their pay does not exactly set the scene for successful teamwork.

It is still very expensive for UK companies to send staff to work abroad. There are many hidden expenses for the employer, and in general it costs them between two and three times the amount they pay the employee in net salary.

For expatriates, remuneration packages that are based on your home salary are increasingly common. Your home salary is the starting point for the package, and then added to this are clearly identified elements, such as location allowances, local tax and a cost-of-living adjustment.

Employers still compensate you for the inconvenience of working away from home. In general, an expatriate allowance is an extra 10 per cent to 15 per cent of salary.

Even though it can seem glamorous to be offered a job abroad, first-time expatriate workers often fail to negotiate a remuneration and benefits package that is comprehensive enough. You may be excited by the opportunity to live outside the British Isles, but take some time to make sure the experience will also be worth your while financially.

Extra costs you will face

Apart from your salary, you need to find out whether your employer will be paying for the relocation. Moving from one house to another even within the same city is an expensive process, but the costs of moving abroad are far heftier.

Some expenses are obvious, such as paying to fly to your destination and to have your belongings transported there, but others are less apparent.

You may have a home in the UK that you will have to maintain without tenants – perhaps the location means it will not be easy to let. Or if you do take on tenants, you could face problems, such as repairs, or unreliable tenants may mean that you do not even end up covering your mortgage costs.

There are hidden accommodation costs too. Even if your expatriate package includes accommodation, you may lose out financially by spending years missing out on the opportunity to own property in London, for example.

If house prices rise at the rate seen in parts of the capital city in the late 1990s, your absence from the property market could cost you tens of thousands of pounds. It could mean you find it impossible to get back into the housing market at the level you left it.

The expense and hassle of buying property mean that it is not usually worth expatriates buying a home abroad if they do not intend to stay in one place for more than two years. But even a rented home you move into in the new country may need furnishing.

If you have dependent family members – a spouse and children – they will have their own additional expenses. In particular children who were educated in state schools in the UK may need expensive private education abroad because of language and syllabus differences.

A spouse who is able to work in the UK is often unable to work abroad because of language or visa difficulties.

Consider your telephone bill. You and your family members are likely to make many more international phone calls than you did in the UK. Your Internet usage will probably be higher too.

Buying groceries may be more expensive than in the UK, particularly if you and your family want to buy favourite imported food items from home. Books and magazines will be a bigger expense if you want to read them in English.

You or members of your family may need to pay for language courses. You might need to buy a new car. And you are likely to want to travel home at least twice a year. Ideally, your employer should bear the cost of these visits.

Consider the cost of living in your new home city. Consultancy William Mercer produces a regular survey that reveals the comparative cost of living in 146 cities around the world. It takes account of the cost of housing, food, clothing and household goods together with transport and entertainment. Multinational companies use the data to help them determine compensation allowances for their expatriate staff.

The cost of living in different cities varies enormously. For instance, it costs about twice as much to live in Tokyo as it does to live in Los Angeles. There are some surprises, too – life in St Petersburg in Russia is more expensive than in London or New York.

Excerpt from the cost of living 2001 survey by William Mercer

Tokyo, Japan	134.0
Moscow, Russia	132.4
Hong Kong	130.0
Beijing, China	124.4
Osaka, Japan	116.7
Shanghai, China	114.3
St Petersburg, Russia	106.5
New York City, US	100.0
Guangzhou, China	97.4
Seoul, South Korea	95.3

Hanoi, Vietnam	94.3
Taipei, Taiwan	92.9
London, England	92.9
Shenzhen, China	90.8
Ho Chi Minh City, Vietnam	90.4
Singapore	86.4
White Plains NY, US	85.5
Tel Aviv, Israel	85.0
San Francisco, US	84.4
Chicago, US	84.3
Kiev, Ukraine	83.8
Beirut, Lebanon	83.8
Buenos Aires, Argentina	83.6
Los Angeles, US	83.4
Miami,US	83.0
Abu Dhabi, United Arab Emirates	82.8

Note: New York = 100

Source: www.wmmercer.com

Reproduced by permission of William M. Mercer.

Levels of expatriate pay and benefit packages

Companies sending staff abroad have different levels of expatriate pay and benefit packages. The highest level is known as full expatriate terms and includes benefits such as a company car, school fees and luxury housing. Mid-level and senior staff at large multinationals would be likely to get these enhanced terms of employment.

Next down the scale are regional expatriate packages, which may have some of the top level benefits but more modest housing, for example. This level of benefit would be given to employees who only move within one region, such as Asia or Europe.

'Local plus' packages are less generous than expatriate deals. They would typically include relocation expenses and a slightly higher salary than locals with the same employer, but may not include housing.

At the lower end of the expatriate remuneration scale are local packages, where staff are on the same terms as local employees.

Just how different an expatriate package is from local terms varies widely depending on the country. In Germany, for example, there may be little difference in salary terms between an expatriate package and a local salary at the same level. In Singapore, expatriate pay may be 50 to 60 per cent more than local pay, but in developing countries, expatriate pay may be several times higher than local pay.

Find out about local taxation

Tax regimes vary widely from country to country, and it is essential to get some specialist advice on taxes before you agree to your new assignment or job.

Even though it is likely that a UK employer sending you on a foreign assignment would offer you a tax-equalized package – meaning you would agree your net pay rather than gross pay – local tax rules may have an impact on other income you may have. You may have rental income from a property you own in the UK, or investment income. This may continue to be taxable in the UK.

As in the UK, residents of many countries face automatic hefty fines if they fail to complete an annual tax return on time. So it is important to know what your responsibilities are in this regard.

Tax and social security systems are so varied that it is essential to get professional advice. Your employer should hopefully give you free access to the firm of accountants used by the company. Or else seek advice from one of the largest accountancy firms such as PricewaterhouseCoopers.

Do not assume anything about tax issues when you are going to work abroad. There are many myths and you can easily get your fingers burned, say accountants.

Offshore investments

From a financial point of view, one of the benefits of working abroad is that you can take advantage of investment tax breaks. If you are not resident in the UK, you can invest your money in an offshore financial centre such as the Isle of Man, the Channel Islands, Luxembourg, Switzerland or Hong Kong. While you continue to be a non-resident, your investments grow free of income tax.

Of course once you return to the UK as a resident, you do become liable to pay tax on those investments, even if they are still held in an offshore centre. However, for the period of time you were abroad, you were able to use money which would have gone to the tax collector to reinvest and therefore grow.

If you have money in a deposit account in the UK at the time you leave for a job abroad, it makes sense to move that money to an offshore savings account. Then, for the duration of your stay abroad, the interest you receive will be gross rather than net of tax.

While you are a non-resident you can also invest in an offshore fund. Similarly, with these investments, you will not be liable to pay tax on the returns you gain.

In this way, you get the benefit of what the industry calls 'gross roll-up', which means the ability to roll over the profit from an investment into the next year's investment without paying tax. You therefore make investment returns on a larger amount of capital than you would have if the returns had been taxed.

But there are some disadvantages to investing offshore. The products offered are usually more expensive than similar products in the UK, for example. And financial regulation is lax in some jurisdictions, which may mean you have fewer rights and recourse if things go wrong.

Health insurance

If you have spent most of your life in the UK, it is easy to assume that basic healthcare at least is always available free. But medical help has to be paid for in the vast majority of countries around the world. And it isn't cheap.

Giving birth in New York, for example, including antenatal and post-natal care, can easily cost $20,000. So private medical insurance, while a luxury in the UK, is essential if you are living abroad. But check with the Department for Work and Pensions to find out which European countries have reciprocal social security agreements with the UK, and which forms you need to have completed to be able to benefit locally.

And it is important that your employer covers you with good local medical insurance which would pay out for any medical expenses at all. A company private medical insurance scheme which is used for UK employees may well be inadequate for expatriates, even though it may technically pay benefits globally.

If it is a UK insurance policy, it should be specifically tailored to expatriates.

Chapter 7

Savings and Investments

Once you have settled into a regular pattern of earning money, it is time to consider your savings and investments. Why do you need to save at all? There are many reasons to save, and they all boil down to one thing – to provide you with money to pay for future needs.

You might come face to face with some of these needs in the very near future, for example, your annual car insurance may be due for renewal in two months' time. Others are further off, such as a deposit for a house; and some may be decades away – retirement, for instance.

For the sake of convenience, these needs can be categorized as short-, medium- and long-term needs. It makes sense to consider the most immediate needs first.

Building up a fund for emergencies

Most financial advisers recommend building up an emergency fund or financial cushion as a first stage of saving money. Ideally this should equate to two or three months' net income. You might dip into it if, say, your washing machine packs up or you have to make expensive but urgent repairs to your car. These are expenses that just can't wait.

Alternatively, if you lost your job unexpectedly, you would have at least three months to find a new one without having to borrow money.

You should keep this emergency fund as easily accessible cash, and certainly not invested in anything risky. An instant access savings account is ideal. When choosing such an account it is worth doing a little market research to find one which pays a competitive rate of interest.

Refer to best buy tables in the financial pages or financial magazines, or use Internet sites, such as *Moneyfacts*, which list the most competitive accounts. Review this at least once a year, and be prepared to switch the account to another savings institution if the interest rates paid have fallen behind competitors.

Once you have this financial buffer zone in place, then you can start thinking about medium-term savings. This is money you might need in a few years' time to pay for home improvements, a new car or your children's higher education costs, for example.

Savings for medium-term needs

Because you are not planning to access this money for five years or more, you can afford to let it grow in a riskier investment vehicle. In general, the riskier an investment, the higher your potential returns are. And risky doesn't mean that you are likely to lose the lot.

Money can grow faster in shares

With stock market funds, for example, high risk simply means that the value of the investment may fluctuate from year to year – but over a period of five years or more it is likely to show good returns.

Equities – or the shares of companies that are traded on the stock market – are a riskier investment than a deposit-based savings account, otherwise known as cash. But over the long term, they have been shown to deliver far higher returns than cash.

According to Barclays Capital, in the 20 years between 1980 and 2000 – taking inflation into account – shares produced real, average annualized returns of 11.8 per cent, compared to 7.7 per cent for UK government bonds, or gilts, and 4.7 per cent for cash investments, such as deposit accounts.

It is important to realize that whether you are investing in collective investments such as unit trusts (see below) or individual company shares, it is over the long term that equities have been shown to produce strong returns.

With funds at least, equity investors should be prepared to keep their money invested for five years at least. And as long as your investment is well diversified – in a general equities fund or with balances spread over different funds – then experience suggests you can expect healthy returns.

You could take up a serious interest in investing in equities and build up your own portfolio of individual shares. But the simplest and most effective way of getting the benefits of investing in equities but not making it a full-time activity is to put your money into investment funds.

What are the financial markets?

Even if you choose to invest in equities in this relatively passive way, you should still equip yourself with a broad understanding of how the financial markets work. This will enable you to make investment decisions and understand investment fund descriptions. Once the financial pages make sense to you, you have a springboard from which to learn more.

The financial markets are an area of utter mystery to many people, even though most have some of their savings invested in them. However, the basic principles are easy to grasp. The financial markets around the world – the London Stock Exchange, the New York Stock Exchange, etc. – are evolved versions of the traditional marketplace.

Imagine a town square where people have come to sell their livestock, food and other wares. The participants in the commercial activity have different roles. Some are the owners selling, others are buyers and some are intermediaries oiling the wheels of the sales process – such as an auctioneer. At each transaction, the seller and the buyer have to agree on a price. The seller wants as much as possible while the buyer want to pay as little as possible.

The financial markets around the world work on this idea. What makes them complicated is the partly the jargon which has grown up with them, and which few outside the market understand, and it is partly the fact that many markets do not actually exist as geographical places. Many of the products that are now traded are also very complex.

Though tangible commodity products such as cocoa beans and gold are still traded, the vast majority of transactions are now in financial products. The stock markets play host to the buying and selling of company shares. A share is a proportion of the capital – or original outlay – on which the company was based. Owning a share signifies part-ownership of that company.

The different financial and securities markets

There are many financial markets besides the stock markets. There are the money markets, where cash is lent and borrowed at mutually agreed rates; the foreign exchange markets, the commodities market, derivatives markets and bond markets. Most of these markets now function electronically, so people participating in them do not have to be in one place physically, but simply need access to the information and communication systems that link them.

Why share prices rise and fall

The prices on financial markets do not stay the same, but constantly fluctuate, reflecting the vitality of the millions of human beings who participate in them every day. What someone is willing to pay for the share of a company – or how much they will pay for the convenience of borrowing £200 000 over three years – depends on many things.

The exact price that another person is willing to sell those items for also depends on a host of factors. You only need to apply your own experience of buying and selling at a car boot sale to become aware of some of those factors. The reason why the whole business of price rises and falls on the stock markets is often complicated to the point of obscurity lies in the vast numbers and cultural diversity of people involved in these markets, the huge geographical areas covered, changing consumer behaviour and political tides.

Economic cycles

An important aspect of the financial markets to understand is how the economy moves in cycles. Just as the seasons of the year follow a pattern of slow then more rapid growth, overheating then dying off and hibernating, so business follows an economic cycle.

In its most extreme form this is what the Government refers to as 'boom and bust'. First comes the boom – a period of frenetic economic activity, when prices are typically rising fast, investors are keen to buy shares and therefore pump more money into companies, and employment is high so consumers are happily spending large amounts of money.

This is eventually followed by a recession when companies and individuals discover they have borrowed more than they can afford, interest rates are high in an attempt by the central bank to get inflation to a lower level, and companies have to lay off workers.

It is the job of Government and the central bank – the Bank of England – to monitor the economic cycle and prevent the extremes that cause the most misery. They do this by finely tuning taxes and interest rates – gently making it more or less attractive to borrow money.

Investment funds

If you stick to investment funds you will not have the tricky task of trying to predict the fortunes of the stock markets. An investment fund is a collective investment. Basically, many different investors pool their money, which a professional fund manager then invests in different shares as they see fit. Returns are shared out equally between the investors.

Unit trusts

There are several different types of investment fund on the market. The most common is a unit trust.

The principle of unit trusts is straightforward. Investors buy units in the trust, and the more people who buy units, the bigger the trust gets. The price of the units changes daily and reflects the value of the assets held in the trust.

There is usually an annual management charge levied on any unit trust, which may be 0.5 per cent to 2 per cent a year. As well as this, there is an initial or upfront charge made when you buy units – this can be up to 6 per cent.

However, there are now numerous discount brokers who are prepared to rebate most or all of this initial charge to you if you buy the investment through them, since most of it is used to pay commission to the intermediary who sells the investment anyway.

Investment trusts

Investment trusts are an older type of collective investment. They are structured as companies rather than trusts and as such issue shares rather than units. They tend to be more volatile than unit trusts, partly because the shares they issue can go up and down in value depending not only on the current value of the assets held by the trust but also depending on the view the market takes of the trust's future performance.

There are different rules governing how investment trusts invest. They are allowed to borrow money. On the one hand, this means if they make good investment decisions they can make even more money, but it also means that they stand to lose more if the shares they buy flop.

OEICs

There is a third main type of collective investment, called an open-ended investment company (OEIC). It is the most recent, having been introduced in 1997. It was designed to combine the best features of investment trusts and unit trusts. Certainly with fund managers the new structure has proved popular, with several large groups including Henderson Investors and HSBC Asset Management having converted their investment trusts and unit trusts to OEICs recently.

Like investment trusts, OEICs are companies that issue shares, but while investment trusts are listed on the stock exchange, OEICs are not.

But in common with unit trusts, they are open-ended. This means they expand according to the demand for their shares. Because of this, their shares can be bought and sold freely, and this avoids the problem experienced by investment trusts of the stock trading at a discount or premium to the net asset value (NAV) of the fund.

From the investors' point of view, probably the best feature of the OEIC structure is one that is borrowed from neither forerunner. OEICs have a single price, rather than a bid-offer spread. This is much easier for new investors to understand.

ISAs

Up to certain annual limits, unit trusts, investment trusts and OEICs can be held tax-free within an Individual Savings Account (ISA). ISAs were introduced in 1999 as the successors to personal equity plans (PEPs) and tax-exempt special savings accounts (TESSAs). An ISA is a tax-free wrapper which can be used to hold a variety of investments including cash, insurance and stocks and shares.

Any capital growth, interest or income generated from investments kept within an ISA is free of income tax and capital gains tax (CGT). Investments within ISAs do not have to be mentioned on tax returns at all.

In the first few years after you take out an equity investment within an ISA, the tax breaks may not add up to much. But an ISA's tax-free status comes into its own years later when the amount of assets held has built up.

This is why it is worth trying to make the most of your annual ISA allowance, because once that tax year has passed without you using your allowance, your entitlement to it has gone.

Mini ISAs and Maxi ISAs

There are two types of ISA wrapper – mini ISAs and maxi ISAs. And there are three categories of investment which can be held within an ISA – cash, stocks and shares or insurance. A mini ISA can only be used to house one of these categories of investment whereas a maxi ISA can be used to hold all three.

In any one tax year, you can either take out up to three separate mini ISAs – one for each category of investment – or you can take out one maxi ISA to hold all three. Although many people have made this mistake, you are not permitted to take out a maxi ISA if you already have a mini ISA in that tax year.

If you choose to take out separate mini ISAs, you have the advantage that you can use a different provider for each. Hopefully this would enable you to find the best value for each category. With a maxi ISA, you have to content yourself with just one provider.

A maxi ISA may not give you the best deal for each element, but the advantage of going into one is that this is the only way you can hold the full £7,000 equities allowance. If you already have a mini cash ISA, for example, you will be deemed to have used up the whole £3,000 cash allowance, leaving correspondingly less to be invested in equities.

So maxi ISAs are particularly suitable for investors who are only interested in stocks and shares investments.

Insurance-based investments

Life assurance companies also offer a range of collective investments. These include endowments, which include an element of life insurance, and with-profit bonds. While many of these may be reasonable value investment products, the trouble with them is that they lack transparency. It is not easy to see exactly how your money is invested and how the investment is performing at any one time.

A selling point for life company investment products such as endowments is that they smooth out the ups and downs of the stock market by withholding profits in good years and use this surplus to make up losses in lean years. But this all makes very little difference to the medium-term investor who has to wait until maturity before they can get at their money anyway.

This lack of transparency often masks high charges, and hinders the comparison of one endowment product to another. Another reason to avoid this type of product is the lack of flexibility. Flexibility is vital in financial planning because despite their efforts, no one can guarantee the course their life will take.

With an endowment, the investor has to wait until maturity to get their hands on the cash to get a good return. Though these policies can be cashed in early if necessary, the amount they yield if this happens cuts the returns considerably and in the early years, the investor may even get less than they had paid in.

Judging and choosing an investment fund

The first way most people judge an investment fund's potential is to look at the historic growth figures of that fund. In their advertising, fund management groups use these often glittering past performance statistics to lure new investors. But at the same time, as they are required to do, they tell us in the small print that past performance is not a guide to future performance.

And they are right. You should not choose to invest in a fund purely because of its past performance. Many small investors do just look at the top performing fund in a league table and go for that. But a lot of top funds have taken big risks to get to that top position, and that type of risk-taking could just as well turn out badly for them in the future.

There are two main reasons why a fund's historical record may be of no relevance to the future. The fund may be under different management or it may have changed in size. If it achieved good performance when it was very small, the techniques it used may not work with a big fund.

And the personalities behind the money play a vital role. Where a fund manager has recently changed, past performance is almost totally irrelevant, and you need to do your research elsewhere.

Past performance data can be a reasonable indicator as to future potential as long as the same fund manager is in place. However, it is not enough simply to check that the fund manager responsible for a period of strong growth is still at their desk. Successful fund managers can retain their job title but in practice be drawn away from investment decision-making. Typically, their time may be taken up with marketing activities.

Try to look for funds run by fund management groups that have demonstrated good performance across a wide range of sectors. Then look for a fund in that range which has a philosophy and risk profile that you are happy with.

Volatility is one way to assess risk. Specialist financial information publication *Moneyfacts* gives a volatility number for each investment fund. However, this measure of short-term fluctuation may give you no clue as to long-term performance.

Small investors can in theory do their own research, though they need a lot of time and access to specialist financial information.

If you don't want to turn investment research into a hobby and give it the time it requires, your best bet is to seek recommendations from an investment broker or independent financial adviser whom you believe is intelligent, hard-working and on the ball.

Trackers

A tracker is an investment fund – a unit trust, OEIC, investment trust or pension fund – which aims to mirror the movements of a particular stock market index – say, the FTSE 100. Trackers are often called passively invested funds as opposed to an actively invested one where the fund's manager uses their investment skills to try to beat a particular index.

Trackers are easy to understand, and can have low charges because they're cheaper to manage. But it's a myth that trackers are safe. A tracker follows an index on its way up, but also has to follow it back down again. When the market is falling, some say active funds do better than trackers.

About risk

Risk can be fun – or frightening. Saving or investing means entrusting your money to someone else – unless you keep it under your mattress.

There are many different types of investment risk. There is always the risk that a banker will run off with your money – but this is a very small risk indeed. However, the risk that shares you buy will fall in value is higher. On the other hand, if you choose a 'safe' option, such as putting your cash in a deposit account, you risk its value becoming eroded by inflation.

Whether you choose a high- or low-risk investment, you should be aware of the risk you are taking.

You may not be a born gambler, but there are good reasons to take some risks with your investments. For example, shares are risky investments. But most experts agree that over periods of five years or more, they are likely to produce higher returns than any other type of investment.

And there are ways you can own shares but keep the risk to a minimum. Owning units in a collective investment fund rather than holding individual shares cuts your risk by avoiding exposure to the fortunes of just one company. Holding the shares for the long term lessens the risk, because this gives the investments enough time to recover from any market crash.

It is important to balance the risks you are taking. As you slowly build up a portfolio – or collection – of savings and investments, you should see it as a whole. A proportion needs to be sheltered from the ups and downs of the stock market – perhaps in a bank deposit account.

Another part might be invested in shares to make sure your money grows as much as it can. And of those shares, some might be in companies which tend to do well when the economy is strong (e.g. retailers), and others in firms that stay steady throughout the economic cycle (e.g. gas and electricity companies).

Comparative risk level of different investments

1 (low risk)	Building society accounts, bank deposits
2.	Government bond fund, with-profits fund
3.	Corporate bond fund
4.	High-yield corporate bond fund
5.	FTSE 100 fund
6.	European smaller companies fund
7.	Major UK shares held individually
8.	Emerging markets fund
9.	Smaller UK shares held individually
10 (high risk)	Warrants, options, individual biotechnology stocks.

How much risk can you take?

To decide which level of risk you are comfortable with, ask yourself some questions.

If your £600 investment dropped in value to just £510 after three months, how would you feel? Would you panic and withdraw the money, or ride out the storm, confident that the loss would be evened out with gains later on?

When will you need the money you are investing? If you need it in eight months to put down as a deposit on a house, then you should probably not risk putting it in any type of stock market investment.

The level of risk you are prepared to take depends partly on personality, and it is partly to do with your age. The longer the period you have until you will need to spend the money you have saved, the more risk you can afford to take.

If you are still in your twenties or thirties and saving for retirement, most of your portfolio might be in shares. But later on as you get close to retiring, the safety of government bonds might be more sensible. And whatever your age, it is sensible to spread your portfolio across investments of different risk classes.

Investment sectors

Investment funds are generally divided into several main investment sectors.

Small caps

These are normally defined as UK companies too small to be in the FTSE 350 index, but with market values of at least £50 million. Investing in small companies is a way of spreading your risk, because within the economic cycle they tend to perform well in phases when blue chips have run out of steam. While investing in small companies individually can be highly risky, smaller companies investment funds are available.

Global investments

Many good investment opportunities are outside the UK. The boom in technology shares, for example, happened primarily in the USA. A global investment fund could have enabled you to share in some of the sector's success. It is also a way of reducing the overall volatility, or ups and downs, in your portfolio.

Emerging markets

The economies of developing countries like Brazil, or financial markets which have recently eased restrictions on foreign investment, such as the Czech Republic are termed emerging markets. They are thought to have far more scope for growth than established economies, and can often capitalize on low local wage costs, for example, and productivity may be higher because of greater motivation.

Many investment funds focus on emerging markets. Some are global, and others stick to a particular region. Emerging markets funds are very high-risk investments.

Split-capital investment trusts

This is a breed of investment trust that has a limited life. These trusts invest as other investment trusts do, but instead of issuing ordinary shares, splits offer a variety of types of share.

Capital and income shares are the most basic types. Income shares benefit from the dividends of all the shares in the trust, while capital shares assume all the capital growth. Other types of share include zero dividend preference shares and stepped preference shares.

Capital shares can offer huge returns – but at a price. They are risky because when the investment trust is wound up, capital shares are last in line for a payout.

VCTs/EIS

Venture capital trusts are one way to share in the growth of small, mainly unquoted companies. Each VCT invests in a number of smaller companies – mostly existing companies or management buyouts, and some early stage companies.

VCTs are high-risk investments, but the risk is spread across a number of businesses. VCTs carry generous tax breaks. (Refer to pages 65–6, Chapter 3 on building a pension.)

Similar tax breaks are available for those investing through the Enterprise Investment Scheme. This was devised as a way of encouraging investment in new and growing UK companies. You can invest up to £100 000 a year in unquoted companies through the scheme, and get income tax relief at a rate of 20 per cent, plus exemption from capital gains tax when the shares are disposed of.

Share trading

If you are buying or selling shares that are already in issue – as opposed to newly issued shares from a recently privatized company – you need to use a stockbroker. Newly issued shares can be bought directly. Ask for a prospectus from the company's sponsor, and follow the instructions. The sponsor is the bank or broker advertising the issue.

You can get a list of stockbrokers from the Association of Private Client Investment Managers and Stockbrokers (020 7247 7080).

Stockbrokers offer different levels of service:

- *Execution-only service* – The broker gives no advice, but just carries out your buying and selling instructions. There is only a dealing fee to pay.
- *Advisory brokerage service* – The broker makes suggestions about whether you should buy or sell particular shares. The final decision is yours. More expensive than execution-only.
- *Discretionary management service* – The broker buys and sells shares for you without waiting for instructions. Most expensive level of service, as it includes a management charge.

To buy shares, you first decide which company's shares you want to deal in, buying or selling, how many and at what price. Then tell your stockbroker by letter or phone, and you will get a contract note detailing the transaction.

You can either hold your own share certificates or hold the shares in your broker's nominee account. Holding them in your broker's account saves having to sign transfer forms and post the certificates.

There is nothing to stop you investing directly in shares with as little as £500. But the costs of dealing are relatively high at this level. You can expect to pay minimum commission of £15, or 1 per cent on deals, and stamp duty of 0.5 per cent is payable on any purchase.

And most financial advisers say if you are going to invest directly in shares you need at least £50 000. This is because it would be hard to spread your risk across enough companies with a smaller amount.

Investment clubs

However, if you are really interested in investing directly in shares, but do not want to commit this level of funds to it, consider joining an investment club or starting your own. Investment clubs are groups of up to 20 people who pool regular savings to invest in the stock market. Most investment clubs are affiliated to ProShare, an organization that produces a manual on starting and running a club (020 7394 5200).

Having control of your investments is a major attraction of share trading. You make the decisions. But good research is essential. Reading the financial pages, relevant magazines and tipsheets can help. Don't buy shares in a company before you have read its annual report and accounts. Many companies now have this information on their web site.

Long-term investment

Long-term investing is primarily meant to provide money for your retirement. For most people, this means some type of pension plan. If you are employed and your employer provides an occupational pension scheme, then that is very likely to be your best option. (Refer to pages 76–82, Chapter 4, employee benefits.)

But if there is no such workplace pension on offer or if you are self-employed, then a personal pension plan is probably suitable. (Refer to pages 109–13, Chapter 5, self-employment.)

ISAs as long-term investments

However, most people want to build up savings for retirement alongside their pension. ISAs are ideal for this. Because they are not taxed, any assets you manage to build up during your working life in ISAs using your annual allowance can be turned into income-producing investments when you retire.

The great advantage of ISAs in retirement is that, unlike income from a pension plan, the income from ISAs is not taxable. Also you have much more flexibility than you do with pension plans. (Refer to pages 137–8.)

When investing for the long term, you can afford to take more risk than for your medium-term investment; although, as with pensions, when you near retirement – say, five years away from it – it is sensible to switch your investments into less volatile vehicles, such as government bonds.

If you have managed to build up a substantial sum over the years, it would be more than slightly irritating to lose a large chunk of it just before you retire.

Glossary

Additional Voluntary Contribution (AVC) an AVC programme is a facility provided by an employer for staff to use to make extra contributions to their occupational pension scheme.

Alternative Investment Market (AIM) London's junior stock market, for smaller and growing quoted companies. Some may subsequently become listed on the London Stock Exchange.

Annuity a financial product, usually from a life insurance company, which gives a guaranteed income for life. Pension lump sums are usually used to buy an annuity.

Benchmark a market index, such as the FTSE 100, or another type of measure against which the performance of an investment fund is compared.

Bid-offer spread the difference between the price at which securities, or units of investment funds, are sold and the price at which they are bought.

Bond an IOU issued by a company or government, which usually pays the holder of the bond a fixed rate of interest. Bonds can often be bought and sold on a stock market.

Buy-to-let mortgage a property loan taken out on a second house or flat that is bought with the intention of letting it to tenants. With careful planning, the mortgage and administrative costs of running the property can be covered by the rental income alone.

Capital gains tax (CGT) a tax that is due on any profit you make when selling an asset, for example, shares, property other than your own home, and antiques. Each taxpayer has an annual

CGT allowance – in the 2001/2002 tax year it is £7500 – and CGT is only payable on gains above that level.

CAT standards   the Government's 'seal of approval' scheme introduced for ISAs and now extended to stakeholder pensions. CAT stands for conditions, terms and access, and financial products have to fulfil certain minimum criteria based on these to win a CAT mark.

Corporate bond unit trusts   funds that invest in fixed-interest securities, including those issued by companies. Best suited to income rather than capital growth investors.

Discount   when the combined shares of an investment trust are trading at a price below the net asset value of the trust, then they are said to be trading at a discount.

Dividend   the distribution of profits paid by a company to the holders of its shares.

Endowment policy   a type of investment plan sold by a life insurance company. It pays out on death or at the end of the term, whichever is sooner.

Equities   shares, as opposed to cash or bonds.

Execution-only broker   an investment broker who gives no advice, but simply carries out the purchase or sale of investments on behalf of the client.

Fixed-interest funds   funds investing in stocks that pay a set return each year, including corporate bonds and government bonds such as UK gilts.

Free-standing additional voluntary contribution (FSAVC) a financial product that is used to top up an occupational pension scheme. As opposed to an AVC policy, which is run alongside the employer's own scheme, an FSAVC policy is sold by external insurance and investment companies.

Gilt-edged securities (gilts) UK government bonds.

Gross income on investments, rates of interest on savings, etc. are described as gross if tax has not yet been deducted from it.

Guaranteed income bond life assurance investment products that promise to pay a fixed rate of interest for a set number of years, as well as returning the original capital to the investor at the end of the term.

Home income plan these products allow homeowners – particularly the elderly – to make use of some of the equity (non-mortgaged market value) in their homes without having to sell their home and move out.

Index tracker fund an investment fund that aims to mirror the movements of a particular market index, such as the FTSE 100.

Individual Savings Account (ISA) tax-free savings and investment vehicle introduced by the Labour Government in 1999. ISAs can be used as wrappers to keep certain investments – cash, equities, bonds and insurance – free of income tax and CGT.

Investment trust a collective investment, or investment fund. It is incorporated as a stock market listed company and exists to invest in shares or other investments. Investors can participate in the growth of its investments by buying shares issued by the trust.

Maxi ISA an ISA that can contain all three investment elements of cash, stocks and shares and insurance. Though not all do have these three elements, all maxi ISAs allow investors to put their full ISA allowance into stocks alone.

Mini ISA an ISA that can only contain one type of investment – cash, stocks and shares or insurance.

Money market fund an investment fund that holds short-term bonds. It pays an interest rate return to its investors.

National Savings the Government's Department for National Savings offers a range of savings and investment schemes to the public in order to raise money to fund government spending. Products include premium bonds, index-linked savings certificates and pensioners' guaranteed income bonds. Some National Savings products are tax-free but others are taxable.

Net asset value the value of all securities held within an investment fund at their current market price.

Open-ended investment company (OEIC) a relatively new type of collective investment, designed to combine the best features of investment trusts and unit trusts. An OEIC issues shares, which are bought and sold at the same price, so there is no bid-offer spread.

Property funds funds invested in commercial or residential property either directly or by investing in the shares of companies in the property sector.

Protected unit trusts investment funds that offer a protected selling price, usually fixed for a certain period. They give investors security in case of a market crash.

Share shares are issued by companies to raise capital. Once these shares are listed on the stock market, the price can go up or down, depending on a number of factors such as the company's profits but also the general economic climate.

Split capital investment trust a type of investment trust that issues different classes of shares, most commonly growth and income shares. Growth shares assume all the growth of the trust's investments while all the dividends are paid to income shareholders.

Stepped preference shares a class of share offered as part of a split capital investment trust. They pay a regular return, with the level fixed in advance. When the trust is wound up, a further gain may be made.

Tax-exempt special savings accounts (TESSAs) these five-year savings plans were abolished when ISAs were introduced in 1999. TESSAs bought before April of that year can run until maturity.

Tracker fund an investment fund that tries to mirror the movements of a particular market index, such as the FTSE 100. These funds are 'passively' managed as opposed to 'actively' managed funds.

Unit trusts a fund of various investments, which can include shares and bonds. Investors buy units of the fund at the current market price, enabling them with a relatively small amount of money to spread their risk across many holdings.

With-profits investments life companies offer this type of investment structure on bonds and endowment policies. Investment volatility is smoothed out by distributing the company's profits relatively evenly in the form of an annual bonus and a terminal bonus when the investment matures.

Yield the return you receive from an investment relative to the price you paid for it. On shares, for example, the yield is calculated by expressing the dividend as a percentage of the price of the share.

Zero-dividend preference shares low-risk class of share offered as part of a split capital investment trust. The shares pay no income but get a fixed payout when the trust is wound up.

Sources of further information

Insurance

Association of British Insurers (ABI)
51 Gresham Street
London EC2V 7HQ

Tel: 020 7600 3333

British Insurers Brokers' Association (BIBA)
BIBA House
14 Bevis Marks
London EC3A 7NT

Tel: 020 7623 9043

Provides details of registered insurance brokers, including specialists in certain types of insurance

Savings and investment

Association of Investment Trust Companies (AITC)
Durrant House
8-13 Chiswell Street
London EC1Y 4YY

Tel: 020 7282 5555

Web site: www.itsonline.co.uk

Publishes information on the performance of investment trusts, and free fact sheets on different aspects of buying investment trusts.

Association of Unit Trusts and Investment Funds (AUTIF)
65 Kingsway
London WC2B 6TD

Tel: 020 8207 1361

Association of Private Client Investment Managers and Stock-brokers (APCIMS)
112 Middlesex Street
London E1 7HY

Tel: 020 7247 7080

APCIMS has a directory of members showing the services they offer.

National Savings
Sales Information Unit
Blackpool FY3 9YP

Debt problems

Citizens' Advice Bureaux

Look in *Yellow Pages* under 'Counselling and Advice'

Consumer Credit Counselling Service

0800 1381111

Self-help packs available by phoning this number, including a guide on how to budget. Standard letters to send to creditors are also included.

Car insurance

Passplus
0115 901 2633

Advanced driving course scheme, whereby motorists completing the course earn a certificate issued by the Driving Standards Agency. With most motor insurers, possession of this certificate gives drivers access to car insurance discounts.

Mortgages

Mortgage brokers

John Charcol: 020 7611 7000 – mortgage brokers
London and Country Mortgages: 01225 870717 – mortgage brokers

Financial information

Moneyfacts: www.moneyfacts.co.uk
Interactive Investor: www.iii.co.uk
Moneynet: www.moneynet.co.uk
Virgin Money: www.virginmoney.com
Financial Times: www.ft.com
Find: www.find.co.uk (gives access to a wide range of financial services companies on the web)
Motley Fool: www.fool.co.uk

Financial advice

IFA Promotion on 0117 971 1177 will give you addresses of three IFAs in your area.

Institute of Financial Planning on 0117 945 2470 has a directory of independent, fee-based certified financial planners, showing their areas of expertise.

Society of Pensions Consultants
St Bartholomew House
92 Fleet Street
London EC4Y 1DH

Can provide a list of independent pensions advisers in your area.

Institute of Chartered Accountants in England and Wales: www.icaew.co.uk – This site will help you find an accountant.

Sort: www.sort.co.uk – offers online independent financial advice for a fee.

Tax

Inland Revenue: www.inlandrevenue.gov.uk

Regulators

Financial Services Authority (FSA)
25 The North Colonnade
Canary Wharf
London E14 5HS

Firms that sell, deal in or advise on investments must be regulated by the FSA. Self-regulatory authorities – PIA, IMRO and SFA – are to be absorbed into the FSA. To check that a firm you are about to use is regulated, call the FSA's Central Register on 0845 606 1234.

Ombudsman's offices

If you have a complaint about a financial firm you have dealt with, you should first go through the firm's own complaints procedure, and then tell the regulator about it. If neither of these channels gives you a satisfactory outcome, go to the relevant ombudsman. Though previously dealt with separately, banking, insurance, investment, share dealing and building society complaints now all come under the umbrella of the Financial Ombudsman Service.

Financial Ombudsman Service
South Quay Plaza
183 Marsh Wall
London E14 9SR

Tel: 020 7404 9944

Pensions Ombudsman
11 Belgrave Road
London SW1V 1RB

Tel: 020 7834 9144

Occupational Pension Advisory Service (OPAS)
11 Belgrave Road
London SW1V 1RB

Tel: 020 7233 8080

Index